Broadway Jazz Standards

Volume 46

Arranged and Produced by
Mark Taylor

Featured Players:

Graham Breedlove–Trumpet
John Desalme–Tenor Sax
Tony Nalker–Piano
Jim Roberts–Bass
Steve Fidyk–Drums

Recorded at Bias Studios, Springfield, Virginia
Bob Dawson, Engineer

HOW TO USE THE CD:

Each song has two tracks:

1) Split Track/Melody

Woodwind, Brass, Keyboard, and **Mallet Players** can use this track as a learning tool for melody style and inflection.

Bass Players can learn and perform with this track – remove the recorded bass track by turning down the volume on the LEFT channel.

Keyboard and **Guitar Players** can learn and perform with this track – remove the recorded piano part by turning down the volume on the RIGHT channel.

2) Full Stereo Track

Soloists or **Groups** can learn and perform with this accompaniment track with the RHYTHM SECTION only.

1 : SPLIT TRACK/MELODY
2 : FULL STEREO TRACK

AIN'T MISBEHAVIN'

FROM AIN'T MISBEHAVIN'

WORDS BY ANDY RAZAF
MUSIC BY THOMAS "FATS" WALLER AND HARRY BROOKS

C VERSION

TO CODA
Ab6 Db7 Eb6 Gb7 Fmi7 Bb7
Eb6 Cmi7 Fmi7 Bb7(b9)
SOLO
Eb6 E°7 Fmi7 F#°7
Gmi7 Bbmi7 Ab6 Db7 Eb6 Gb7 Fmi7 Bb7
1.
G7 C7 F7 Bb7(b9)
2.
Eb6 Ab7 D7(b9) G+7
Cmi Ab7/C F7/C C7
Bb6/F Db7 Cmi7 F7 Bb7 C7 F7 Bb7(b9)
Eb6 E°7 Fmi7 F#°7 Gmi7 Bbmi7 Ab6 Db9
D.S. AL CODA
Eb6 Gb7 Fmi7 Bb7 Eb6 Ab7 D7(b9) G+7
CODA
Eb6/9 Db7 D7(b9) Eb6/9

CD

3: SPLIT TRACK/MELODY
4: FULL STEREO TRACK

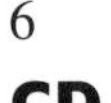

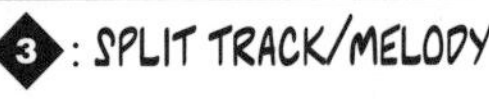

GET ME TO THE CHURCH ON TIME

FROM MY FAIR LADY

WORDS BY ALAN JAY LERNER
MUSIC BY FREDERICK LOEWE

C VERSION

FAST SWING

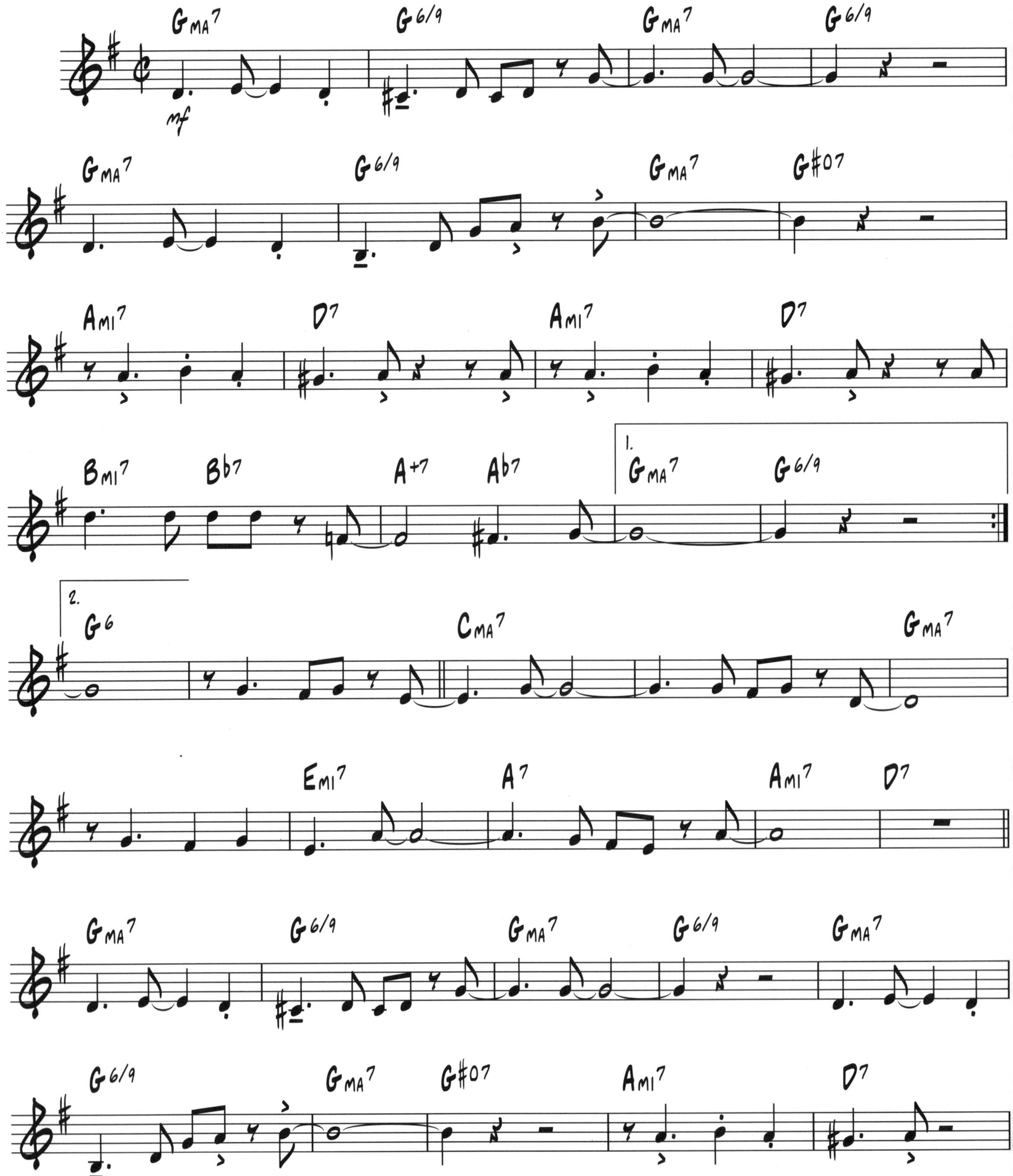

BMI7 E7(b9) AMI7 CMI7 F7

TO CODA

BMI7 Bb7 AMI7 G6/B CMA7 A7/C# D7SUS D7(b9)

G6 SOLO BREAK

SOLO

GMA7 G6/9 GMA7 G6/9

GMA7 G6/9 GMA7 G#O7 AMI7 D7 AMI7 D7

BMI7 Bb7 A+7 Ab7 1. GMA7 G6/9 2. G6 CMA7

GMA7 EMI7 A7 AMI7 D7 GMA7 G6/9

GMA7 G6/9 GMA7 G6/9 GMA7 G#O7 AMI7 D7

BMI7 E7(b9) AMI7 CMI7 F7 BMI7 Bb7

D.C. AL CODA

TAKE REPEAT

AMI7 G6/B CMA7 A7/C# D7SUS D7(b9) D7SUS D7(b9)

CODA

G6 Ab6/9 GMA7

CD

5: SPLIT TRACK/MELODY

6: FULL STEREO TRACK

I LOVE PARIS

FROM CAN-CAN

FROM HIGH SOCIETY

WORDS AND MUSIC
BY COLE PORTER

TO CODA
DMI7
3
G7SUS
G7(b9)
C6
DMI7(b5)
G+7
SOLO
CMI
Ab/C
CMI6
CMI7
CMI(MA7)
CMI7
CMI6
Ab/C
CMI
CMI/Bb
A°7
Ab7
G7SUS
G7(b9)
DMI7(b5)
G7(b9)
DMI7(b5)
G7(b9)
DMI7(b5)
Ab7
G7SUS
G+7(b9)
CMI6
CMI
G7SUS
CMA7
FMA7/C
CMA7
FMA7/C
F#MI7(b5)
FMA7
EMI7
A7
DMI7
G7
FMA7
F#°7
B7(b9)
EMI7
FMA7
EMI7
A7
D.S. AL CODA
DMI7
G7SUS
G7(b9)
C6
DMI7(b5)
G+7
CODA
CMI
Ab/C
CMI6
CMI7
CMI(MA7)
CMI7
CMI6
Ab/C
CMI6/9

CD

IT NEVER ENTERED MY MIND

FROM HIGHER AND HIGHER

WORDS LORENZ HART
MUSIC BY RICHARD RODGERS

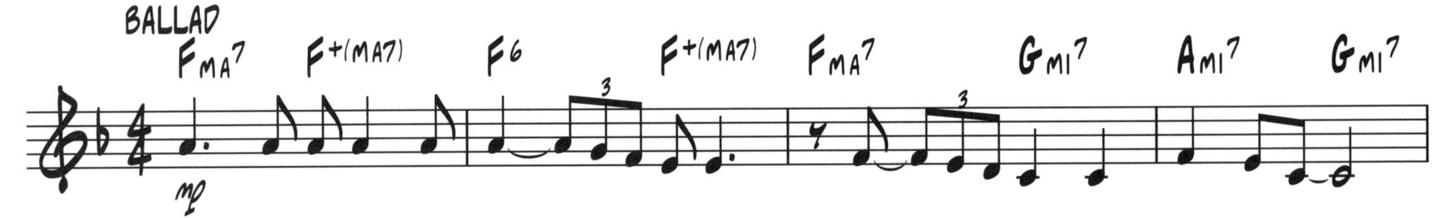

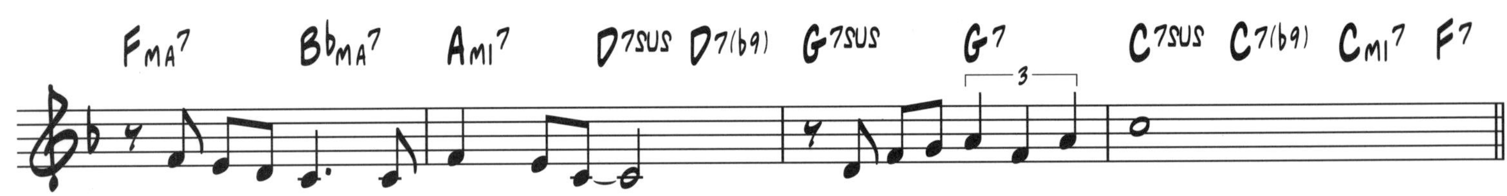

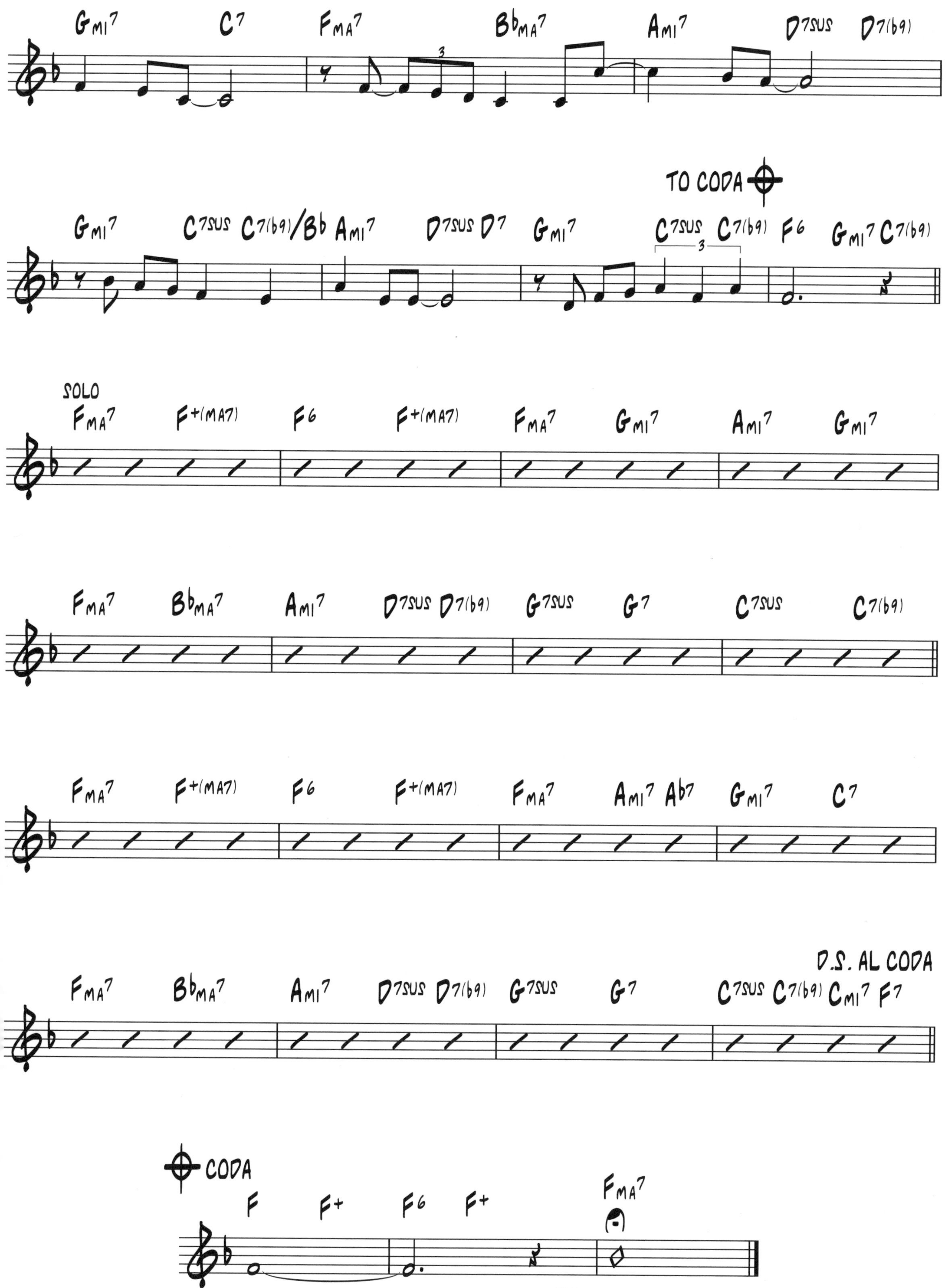
GMI7 C7 FMA7 BbMA7 AMI7 D7SUS D7(b9)
TO CODA
GMI7 C7SUS C7(b9)/Bb AMI7 D7SUS D7 GMI7 C7SUS C7(b9) F6 GMI7 C7(b9)
SOLO
FMA7 F+(MA7) F6 F+(MA7) FMA7 GMI7 AMI7 GMI7
FMA7 BbMA7 AMI7 D7SUS D7(b9) G7SUS G7 C7SUS C7(b9)
FMA7 F+(MA7) F6 F+(MA7) FMA7 AMI7 Ab7 GMI7 C7
D.S. AL CODA
FMA7 BbMA7 AMI7 D7SUS D7(b9) G7SUS G7 C7SUS C7(b9) CMI7 F7
CODA
F F+ F6 F+ FMA7
RIT.

CD

11: SPLIT TRACK/MELODY
12: FULL STEREO TRACK

MAKE SOMEONE HAPPY

FROM DO RE MI

WORDS BY BETTY COMDEN AND ADOLPH GREEN
MUSIC BY JULE STYNE

C VERSION

TO CODA
FMI7 GMI7 AbMA7 Bb7SUS Bb7(b9) G+7(b9) Gb13 FMI9 Bb13(b9)
3
SOLO
Eb Eb+ Eb6 EbMA7 Eb Eb+ Eb6 EbMA7
BbMI7 BbMI(MA7) BbMI7 BbMI6 BbMI7 Eb7SUS Eb7(b9)
AbMA7 Ab+ Ab6 AbMA7 AbMI7 Db7 Bb7(b9)
1.
EbMA7 GMI7 C7(b9) FMI7 Bb13(b9)
2.
D.S. AL CODA
EbMA7 Db7 C7SUS Ab7 GMI7 GMI(MA7) GMI7 C7
CODA
AbMA7 Gb7 FMI7 Bb7SUS AbMA7 Gb7 FMI7 Bb7SUS
AbMA7 Gb7 FMI7 EMA7(b5) EbMA7(b5)

CD

13: SPLIT TRACK/MELODY
14: FULL STEREO TRACK

OLD DEVIL MOON

FROM FINIAN'S RAINBOW

WORDS BY E.Y. HARBURG
MUSIC BY BURTON LANE

C VERSION

LATIN

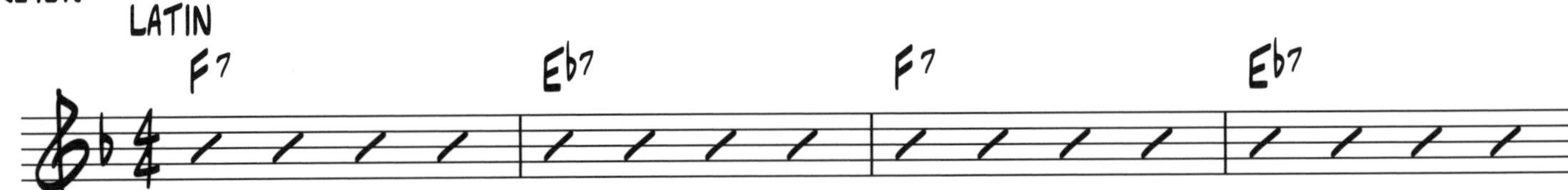

TO CODA
LATIN
AMI7
D7
GMI7
C7
F7
Eb7
LATIN
SOLO
F7
Eb7
F7
Eb7
F7
Eb7
F7
DbMA7
CMI7
F7(b9)
SWING
BbMA7
Eb7(b5)
AbMI7
Db7
Gb6
C7
F7
Eb7
1.
F7
Eb7
DMA7
DMI7
G7
GMI7
C+7
2.
F7
Eb7
F7
Eb7
AMI7
D7
GMI7
C7
F7
Eb7
D.S. AL CODA
TAKE 2ND ENDING
CODA
F7
Eb7
F7
Eb7
F7
Eb7
F7(b5)

CD

15: SPLIT TRACK/MELODY
16: FULL STEREO TRACK

SMALL WORLD

FROM GYPSY

WORDS BY STEPHEN SONDHEIM
MUSIC BY JULE STYNE

C VERSION

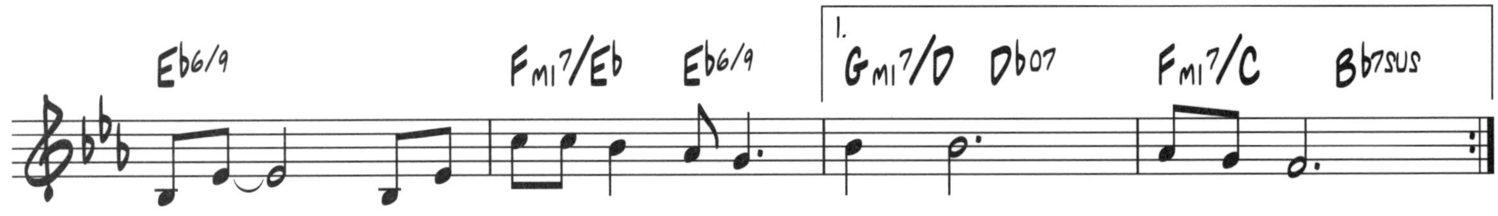

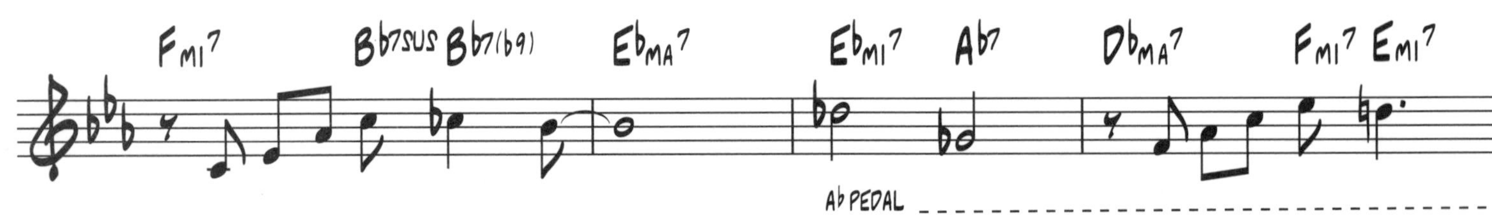

Eb6/9 Fmi7/Eb Eb6/9 Gmi7/D Db07
3
Fmi7/C Bb7sus Gmi7 C7sus C7
TO CODA
F7sus F7 Bb7sus Bb7 Eb6/9 E6/9
SOLO
Eb6/9 Fmi7/Eb Eb6/9 Fmi7/Eb Eb6/9 B7(b5) Bb7sus
1.
Eb6/9 Fmi7/Eb Eb6/9 Gmi7/D Db07 Fmi7/C Bb7sus
2.
Gmi7 C7sus C7
D.S. AL CODA
CODA
Eb6/9
E6/9 Eb6/9 E6/9 Ema7(b5) Ebma7(b5)
RIT.

CD

17 : SPLIT TRACK/MELODY

18 : FULL STEREO TRACK

TILL THERE WAS YOU

FROM MEREDITH WILLSON'S THE MUSIC MAN

BY MEREDITH WILLSON

SOLO
Ebma7
E°7
Fmi7
Abmi7
Db7
Ebma7
F#°7
Fmi7
Bb7
1.
Gmi7
Gb7
Fmi7
Bb7
2.
Eb6
Db7
D7(b9)
Ebma7
Abma7
A°7
Ebma7/Bb
Gmi7
C7(b9)
Fmi7
Cmi7
F7
Fmi7
Bb+7
Ebma7
E°7
Fmi7
Abmi7
Db7
Ebma7
F#°7
Fmi7
Bb7
Eb6
Db7
D7(b9)
Ebma7
D.S. AL CODA
CODA
Eb6
Cmi7
Fmi7
Bb7
E7
Ebma7

CD

19 : SPLIT TRACK/MELODY
20 : FULL STEREO TRACK

TOO CLOSE FOR COMFORT

FROM THE MUSICAL MR. WONDERFUL

WORDS AND MUSIC BY JERRY BOCK,
LARRY HOLOFCENER AND GEORGE WEISS

C VERSION

SWING

mf

C6/9 B+7 Emi7(b5) A7

Dmi7(b5) G7(b9) Cma7 | 1. Ami7 Dmi7 G7(b9)

2. Ab°7 Gmi7 C7(b9) F7 F#°7

C6/G Gmi7 C7(b9) F7 F#°7

C6/G Ab7 G7sus G7(b9) 𝄋 C6/9 B+7

Emi7(b5) A7 Dmi7(b5) G7(b9) Cma7

Ab°7 Gmi7 C7(b9) F7 F#°7

TO CODA

Ami7(b5) D7(b9) Ab7 G7(b9) C6/9

SOLO BREAK
SOLO (2 CHORUSES)
C6/9
B+7
Emi7(b5)
A7
Dmi7(b5)
G7(b9)
1.
C6
Ami7
Dmi7
G7(b9)
2.
C6
Abo7
Gmi7
C7(b9)
F7
F#o7
C6/G
Gmi7
C7(b9)
F7
F#o7
C6/G
Ab7
G7SUS
G7(b9)
C6/9
B+7
Emi7(b5)
A7
Dmi7(b5)
G7(b9)
C6
Abo7
Gmi7
C7(b9)
F7
F#o7
Ami7(b5)
D7(b9)
D.S. AL CODA
Ab7
G7(b9)
C6/9
G7SUS
G7(b9)
CODA
Cma13(#11)

CD

7 : SPLIT TRACK/MELODY
8 : FULL STEREO TRACK

C VERSION

I'VE GROWN ACCUSTOMED TO HER FACE

FROM MY FAIR LADY

WORDS BY ALAN JAY LERNER
MUSIC BY FREDERICK LOEWE

CD
7 : SPLIT TRACK/MELODY
8 : FULL STEREO TRACK

B♭ VERSION

I'VE GROWN ACCUSTOMED TO HER FACE

FROM MY FAIR LADY

WORDS BY ALAN JAY LERNER
MUSIC BY FREDERICK LOEWE

CD

1 : SPLIT TRACK/MELODY

2 : FULL STEREO TRACK

AIN'T MISBEHAVIN'

FROM AIN'T MISBEHAVIN'

WORDS BY ANDY RAZAF
MUSIC BY THOMAS "FATS" WALLER AND HARRY BROOKS

B♭ VERSION

MED. SWING

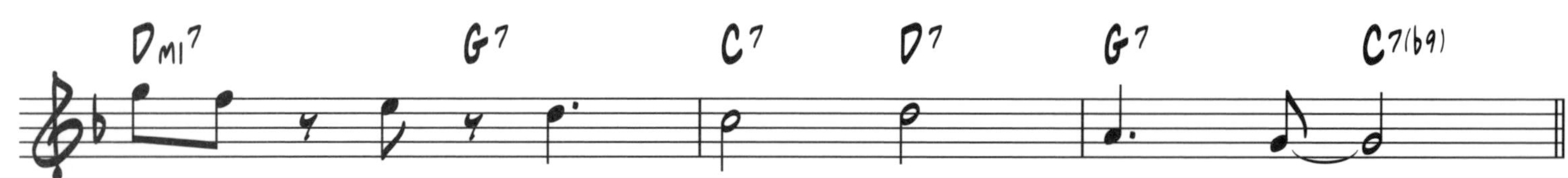

TO CODA
Bb6 Eb7 F6 Ab7 Gmi7 C7
F6 Dmi7 Gmi7 C7(b9)
SOLO
F6 F#o7 Gmi7 G#o7
Ami7 Cmi7 Bb6 Eb7 F6 Ab7 Gmi7 C7
1.
A7 D7 G7 C7(b9)
2.
F6 Bb7 E7(b9) A+7
Dmi Bb7/D G7/D D7
C6/G Eb7 Dmi7 G7 C7 D7 G7 C7(b9)
F6 F#o7 Gmi7 G#o7 Ami7 Cmi7 Bb6 Eb7
D.S. AL CODA
F6 Ab7 Gmi7 C7 F6 Bb7 E7(b9) A+7
CODA
F6/9 Eb7 E7(b9) F6/9

CD

GET ME TO THE CHURCH ON TIME

FROM MY FAIR LADY

WORDS BY ALAN JAY LERNER
MUSIC BY FREDERICK LOEWE

FAST SWING

C♯mi7
F♯7(♭9)
Bmi7
Dmi7
G7
C♯mi7
C7
Bmi7
A6/C♯
Dma7
B7/D♯
E7sus
TO CODA
E7(♭9)
A6 SOLO BREAK
SOLO
Ama7
A6/9
Ama7
A6/9
Ama7
A6/9
Ama7
A♯o7
Bmi7
E7
Bmi7
E7
C♯mi7
C7
B+7
B♭7
1.
Ama7
A6/9
2.
A6
Dma7
Ama7
F♯mi7
B7
Bmi7
E7
Ama7
A6/9
Ama7
A6/9
Ama7
A6/9
Ama7
A♯o7
Bmi7
E7
C♯mi7
F♯7(♭9)
Bmi7
Dmi7
G7
C♯mi7
C7
D.C. AL CODA
TAKE REPEAT
Bmi7
A6/C♯
Dma7
B7/D♯
E7sus
E7(♭9)
E7sus
E7(♭9)
CODA
A6
B♭6/9
Ama7

CD

- 5 : SPLIT TRACK/MELODY
- 6 : FULL STEREO TRACK

I LOVE PARIS

FROM CAN-CAN
FROM HIGH SOCIETY

WORDS AND MUSIC
BY COLE PORTER

TO CODA
EMI7 A7SUS A7(b9) D6 EMI7(b5) A+7
SOLO
DMI Bb/D DMI6 DMI7 DMI(MA7) DMI7 DMI6 Bb/D
DMI DMI/C B°7 Bb7 A7SUS A7(b9)
EMI7(b5) A7(b9) EMI7(b5) A7(b9)
EMI7(b5) Bb7 A7SUS A+7(b9) DMI6 DMI A7SUS
DMA7 GMA7/D DMA7 GMA7/D
G#MI7(b5) GMA7 F#MI7 B7 EMI7 A7
GMA7 G#°7 C#7(b9) F#MI7 GMA7 F#MI7 B7
D.S. AL CODA
EMI7 A7SUS A7(b9) D6 EMI7(b5) A+7
CODA
DMI Bb/D DMI6 DMI7 DMI(MA7) DMI7 DMI6 Bb/D DMI6/9

CD

9 : SPLIT TRACK/MELODY
10 : FULL STEREO TRACK

IT NEVER ENTERED MY MIND

FROM HIGHER AND HIGHER

WORDS LORENZ HART
MUSIC BY RICHARD RODGERS

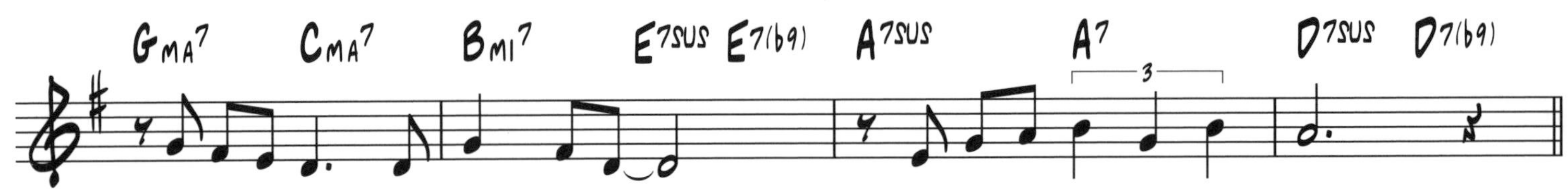

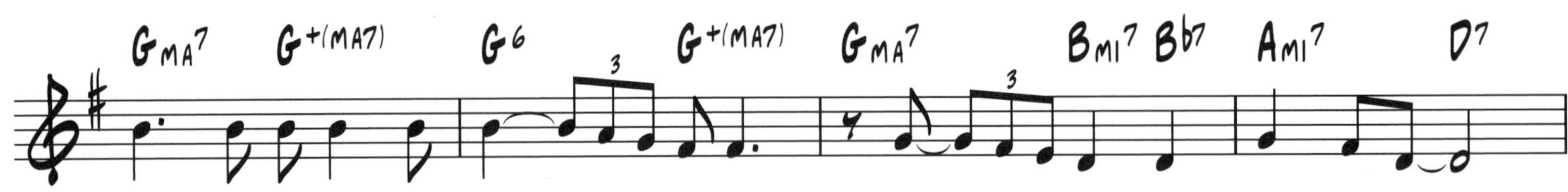

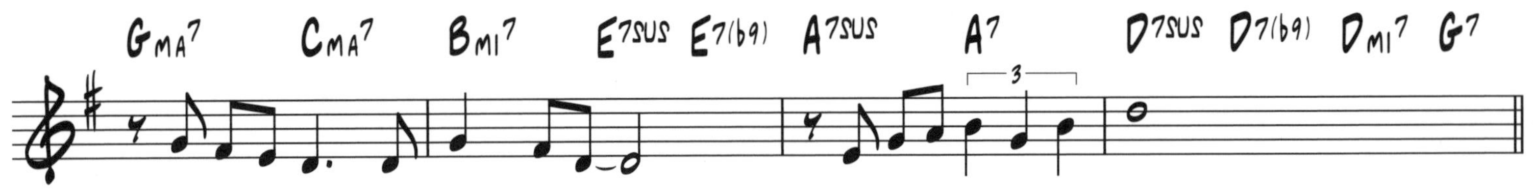

AMI7 D7 GMA7 CMA7 BMI7 E7SUS E7(b9)
TO CODA
AMI7 D7SUS D7(b9)/C BMI7 E7SUS E7 AMI7 D7SUS D7(b9) G6 AMI7 D7(b9)
SOLO
GMA7 G+(MA7) G6 G+(MA7) GMA7 AMI7 BMI7 AMI7
GMA7 CMA7 BMI7 E7SUS E7(b9) A7SUS A7 D7SUS D7(b9)
GMA7 G+(MA7) G6 G+(MA7) GMA7 BMI7 Bb7 AMI7 D7
D.S. AL CODA
GMA7 CMA7 BMI7 E7SUS E7(b9) A7SUS A7 D7SUS D7(b9) DMI7 G7
CODA
G G+ G6 G+ GMA7
RIT.

CD

11 : SPLIT TRACK/MELODY
12 : FULL STEREO TRACK

MAKE SOMEONE HAPPY

FROM DO RE MI

WORDS BY BETTY COMDEN AND ADOLPH GREEN
MUSIC BY JULE STYNE

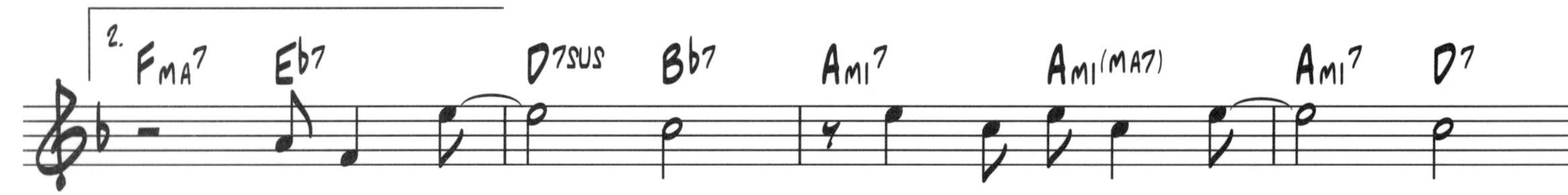

TO CODA
GMI7 AMI7 Bb MA7 C7SUS C7(b9) A+7(b9) Ab13 GMI9 C13(b9)
3
SOLO
F F+ F6 FMA7 F F+ F6 FMA7
CMI7 CMI(MA7) CMI7 CMI6 CMI7 F7SUS F7(b9)
BbMA7 Bb+ Bb6 BbMA7 BbMI7 Eb7 C7(b9)
1.
FMA7 AMI7 D7(b9) GMI7 C13(b9)
D.S. AL CODA
2.
FMA7 Eb7 D7SUS Bb7 AMI7 AMI(MA7) AMI7 D7
CODA
BbMA7 Ab7 GMI7 C7SUS BbMA7 Ab7 GMI7 C7SUS
BbMA7 Ab7 GMI7 F#MA7(b5) FMA7(b5)

CD

13 : SPLIT TRACK/MELODY

14 : FULL STEREO TRACK

OLD DEVIL MOON

FROM FINIAN'S RAINBOW

WORDS BY E.Y. HARBURG
MUSIC BY BURTON LANE

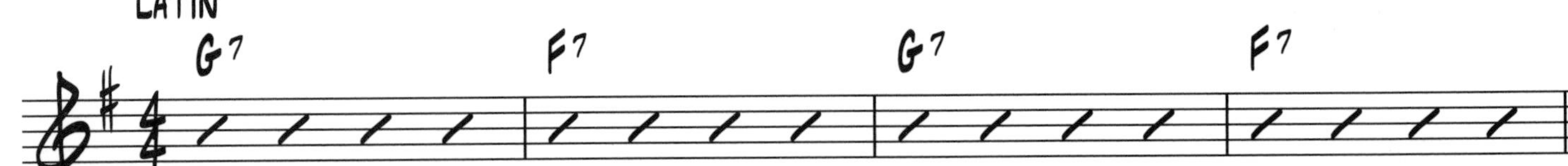

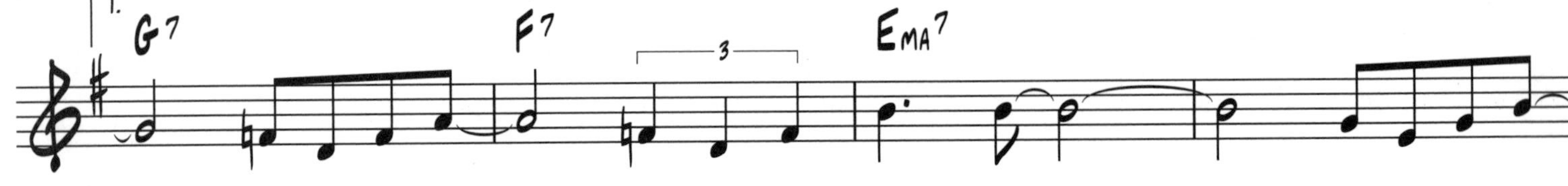

TO CODA
LATIN
Bmi7 E7 Ami7 D7 G7 F7
LATIN
SOLO
G7 F7 G7 F7
G7 F7 G7 Ebma7 Dmi7 G7(b9)
SWING
Cma7 F7(b5) Bbmi7 Eb7
Ab6 D7 G7 F7
1.
G7 F7
Ema7 Emi7 A7 Ami7 D+7
2.
G7 F7 G7 F7
D.S. AL CODA
TAKE 2ND ENDING
Bmi7 E7 Ami7 D7 G7 F7
CODA
G7 F7 G7 F7
G7 F7 G7(b5)

CD

15: SPLIT TRACK/MELODY

16: FULL STEREO TRACK

SMALL WORLD

FROM GYPSY

WORDS BY STEPHEN SONDHEIM
MUSIC BY JULE STYNE

B♭ VERSION

SOFT LATIN

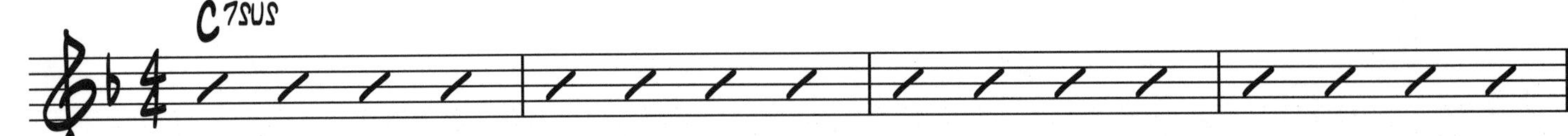

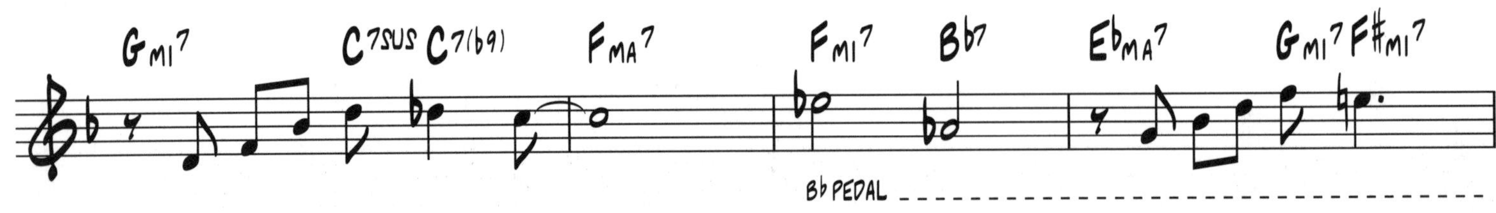

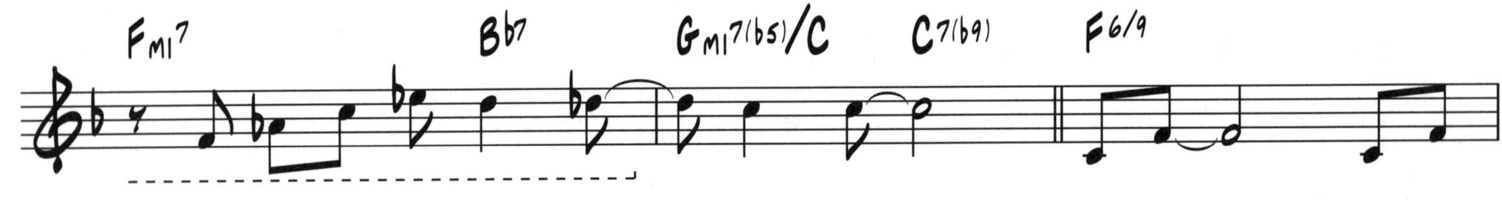

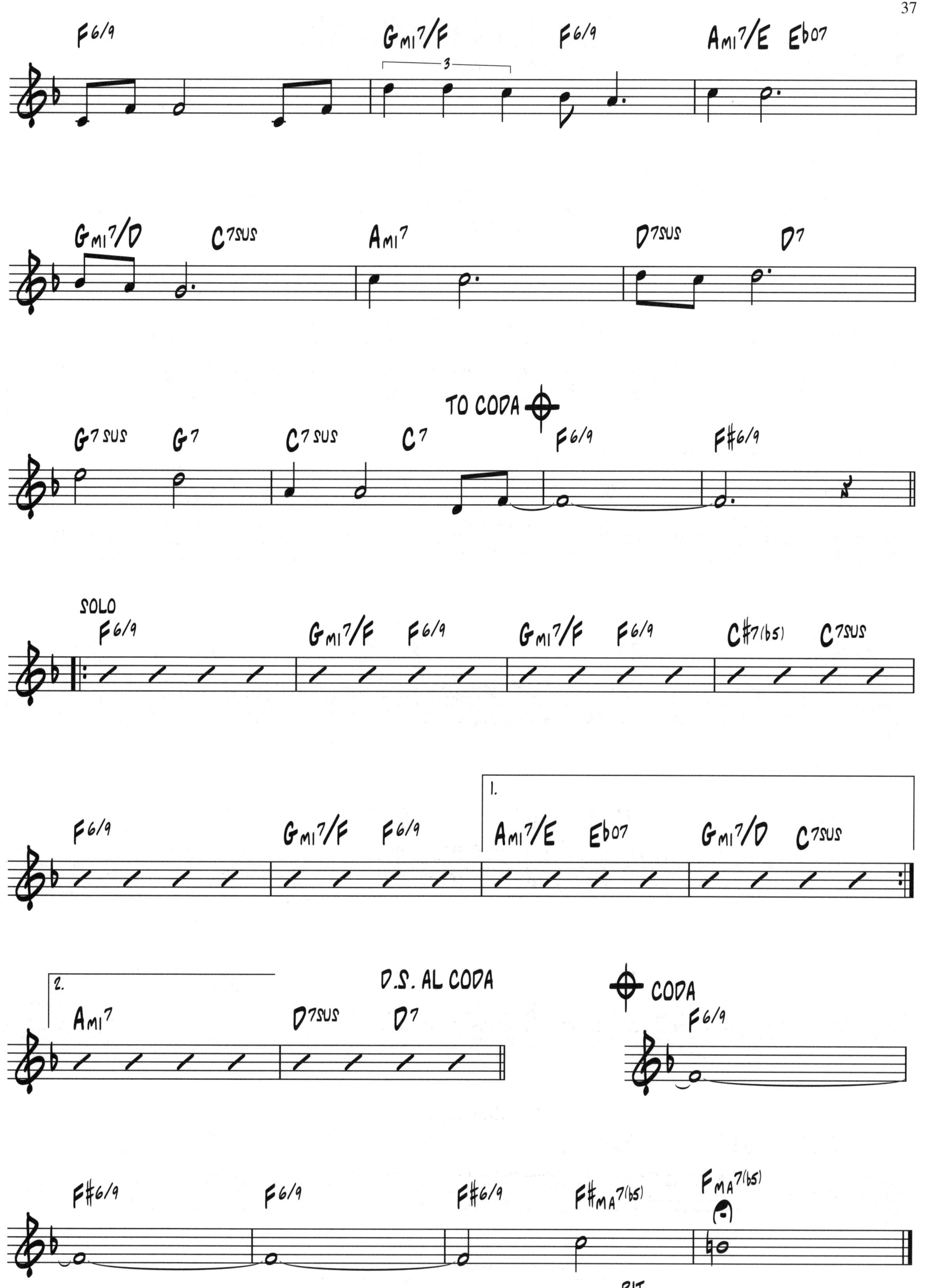
F6/9
Gmi7/F
F6/9
Ami7/E
Eb°7
Gmi7/D
C7sus
Ami7
D7sus
D7
TO CODA
G7 sus
G7
C7 sus
C7
F6/9
F#6/9
SOLO
F6/9
Gmi7/F
F6/9
Gmi7/F
F6/9
C#7(b5)
C7sus
F6/9
Gmi7/F
F6/9
1.
Ami7/E
Eb°7
Gmi7/D
C7sus
2.
Ami7
D7sus
D7
D.S. AL CODA
CODA
F6/9
F#6/9
F6/9
F#6/9
F#ma7(b5)
Fma7(b5)
RIT.

CD

17: SPLIT TRACK/MELODY
18: FULL STEREO TRACK

TILL THERE WAS YOU

FROM MEREDITH WILLSON'S THE MUSIC MAN

BY MEREDITH WILLSON

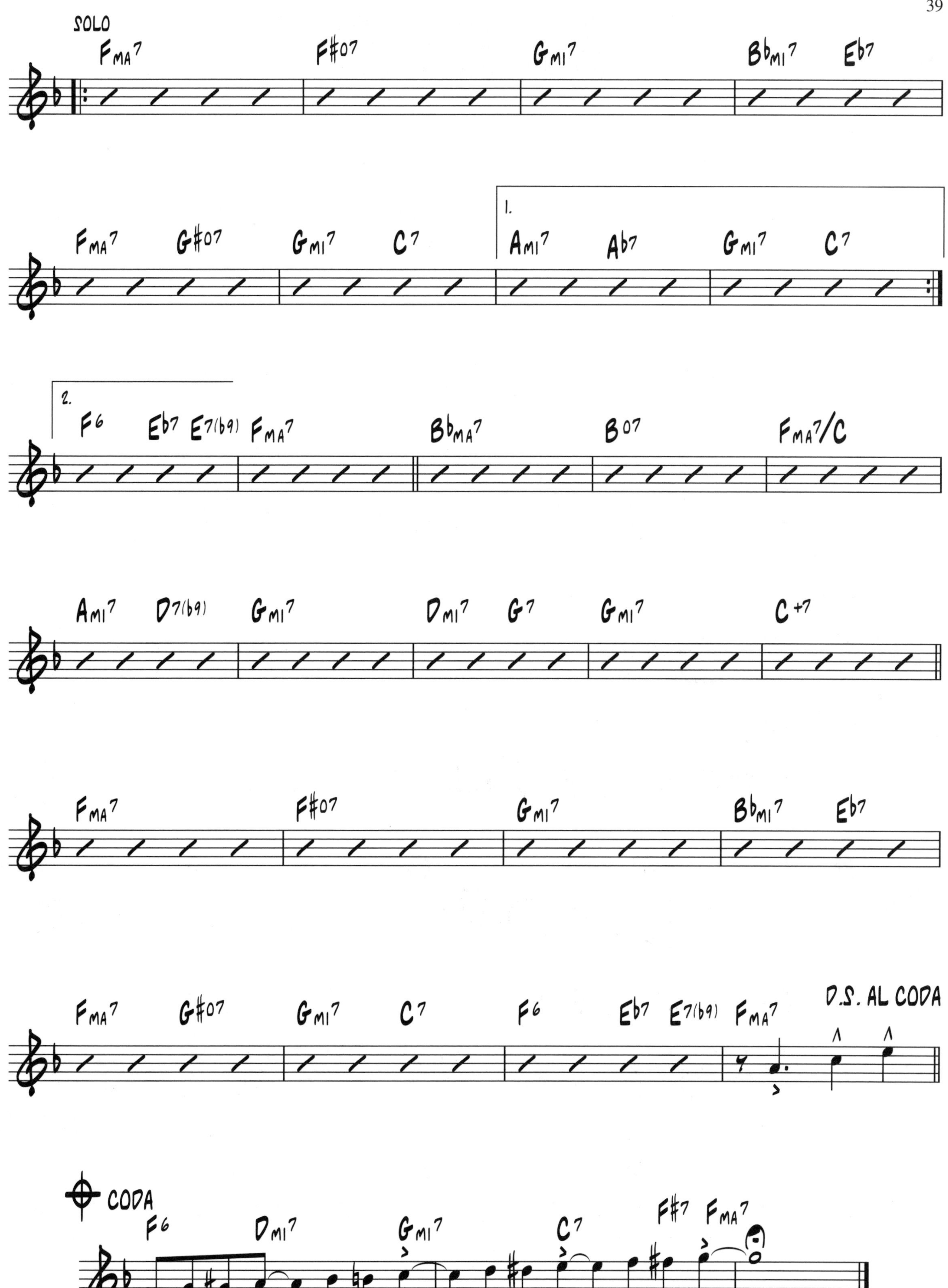
SOLO
FMA7
F#o7
GMI7
BbMI7
Eb7
FMA7
G#o7
GMI7
C7
1.
AMI7
Ab7
GMI7
C7
2.
F6
Eb7
E7(b9)
FMA7
BbMA7
Bo7
FMA7/C
AMI7
D7(b9)
GMI7
DMI7
G7
GMI7
C+7
FMA7
F#o7
GMI7
BbMI7
Eb7
FMA7
G#o7
GMI7
C7
F6
Eb7
E7(b9)
FMA7
D.S. AL CODA
CODA
F6
DMI7
GMI7
C7
F#7
FMA7

CD

19 : SPLIT TRACK/MELODY
20 : FULL STEREO TRACK

TOO CLOSE FOR COMFORT

FROM THE MUSICAL MR. WONDERFUL

WORDS AND MUSIC BY JERRY BOCK, LARRY HOLOFCENER AND GEORGE WEISS

SOLO BREAK
SOLO (2 CHORUSES)
D6/9
C#+7
F#MI7(b5)
B7
EMI7(b5)
A7(b9)
1.
D6
BMI7
EMI7
A7(b9)
2.
D6
Bbo7
AMI7
D7(b9)
G7
G#o7
D6/A
AMI7
D7(b9)
G7
G#o7
D6/A
Bb7
A7SUS
A7(b9)
D6/9
C#+7
F#MI7(b5)
B7
EMI7(b5)
A7(b9)
D6
Bbo7
AMI7
D7(b9)
G7
G#o7
BMI7(b5)
E7(b9)
Bb7
A7(b9)
D6/9
A7SUS
A7(b9)
D.S. AL CODA
CODA
DMA13(#11)

CD

AIN'T MISBEHAVIN'

FROM AIN'T MISBEHAVIN'

WORDS BY ANDY RAZAF
MUSIC BY THOMAS "FATS" WALLER AND HARRY BROOKS

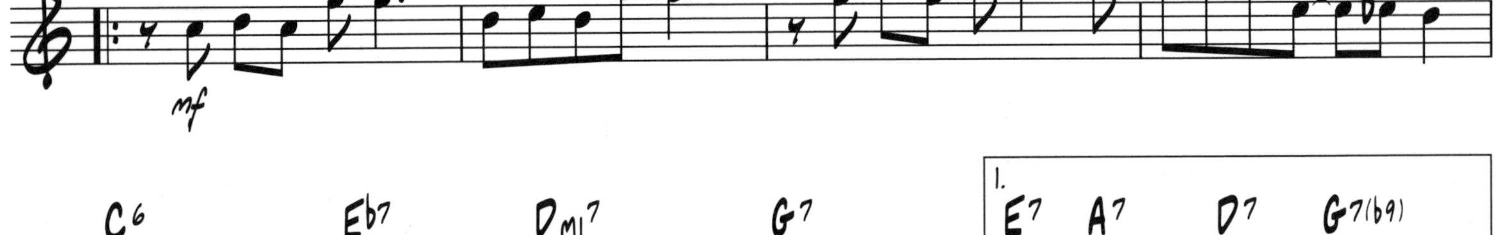

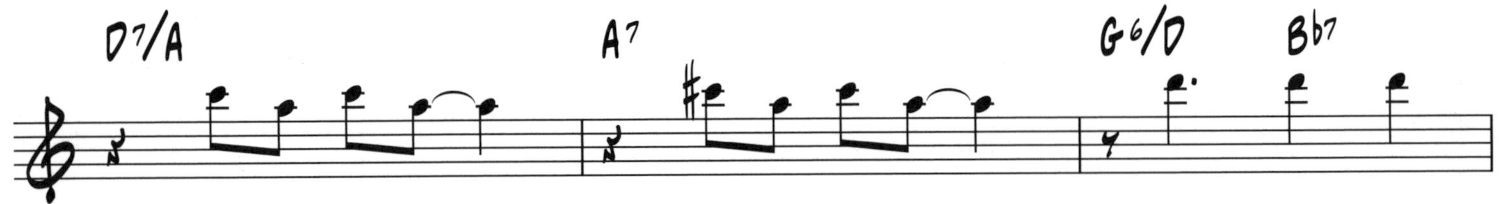

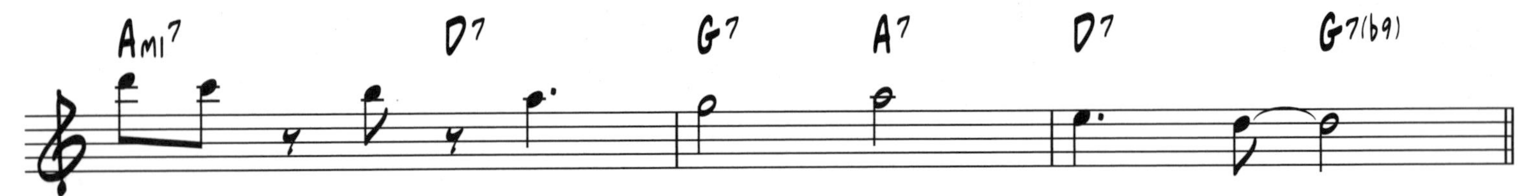

F6
Bb7
C6
Eb7
Dmi7
G7
TO CODA
C6
Ami7
Dmi7
G7(b9)
SOLO
C6
C#o7
Dmi7
D#o7
Emi7
Gmi7
F6
Bb7
C6
Eb7
Dmi7
G7
1.
E7
A7
D7
G7(b9)
2.
C6
F7
B7(b9)
E+7
Ami
F7/A
D7/A
A7
G6/D
Bb7
Ami7
D7
G7
A7
D7
G7(b9)
C6
C#o7
Dmi7
D#o7
Emi7
Gmi7
F6
Bb7
D.S. AL CODA
C6
Eb7
Dmi7
G7
C6
F7
B7(b9)
E+7
CODA
C6/9
Bb7
B7(b9)
C6/9

CD

3 : SPLIT TRACK/MELODY
4 : FULL STEREO TRACK

GET ME TO THE CHURCH ON TIME

FROM MY FAIR LADY

WORDS BY ALAN JAY LERNER
MUSIC BY FREDERICK LOEWE

G#MI7 C#7(b9) F#MI7 AMI7 D7
G#MI7 G7 F#MI7 E6/G# AMA7 F#7/A# B7SUS B7(b9)
TO CODA
E6 SOLO BREAK
SOLO
EMA7 E6/9 EMA7 E6/9
EMA7 E6/9 EMA7 E#O7 F#MI7 B7 F#MI7 B7
G#MI7 G7 F#+7 F7
1.
EMA7 E6/9
2.
E6 AMA7
EMA7 C#MI7 F#7 F#MI7 B7 EMA7 E6/9
EMA7 E6/9 EMA7 E6/9 EMA7 E#O7 F#MI7 B7
G#MI7 C#7(b9) F#MI7 AMI7 D7 G#MI7 G7
D.C. AL CODA
TAKE REPEAT
F#MI7 E6/G# AMA7 F#7/A# B7SUS B7(b9) B7SUS B7(b9)
CODA
E6 F6/9 EMA7

CD

I LOVE PARIS

FROM CAN-CAN
FROM HIGH SOCIETY

WORDS AND MUSIC
BY COLE PORTER

E♭ VERSION

SOFT SAMBA

TO CODA
BMI7
E7SUS E7(b9)
A6
BMI7(b5) E+7
SOLO
AMI F/A AMI6 AMI7 AMI(MA7) AMI7 AMI6 F/A
AMI AMI/G F#O7 F7 E7SUS E7(b9)
BMI7(b5) E7(b9) BMI7(b5) E7(b9)
BMI7(b5) F7 E7SUS E+7(b9) AMI6 AMI E7SUS
AMA7 DMA7/A AMA7 DMA7/A
D#MI7(b5) DMA7 C#MI7 F#7 BMI7 E7
DMA7 D#O7 G#7(b9) C#MI7 DMA7 C#MI7 F#7
D.S. AL CODA
BMI7 E7SUS E7(b9) A6 BMI7(b5) E+7
CODA
AMI F/A AMI6 AMI7 AMI(MA7) AMI7 AMI6 F/A AMI6/9

CD

IT NEVER ENTERED MY MIND

FROM HIGHER AND HIGHER

WORDS LORENZ HART
MUSIC BY RICHARD RODGERS

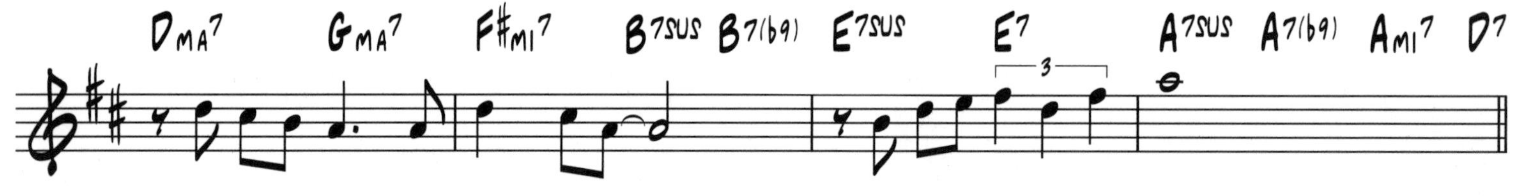

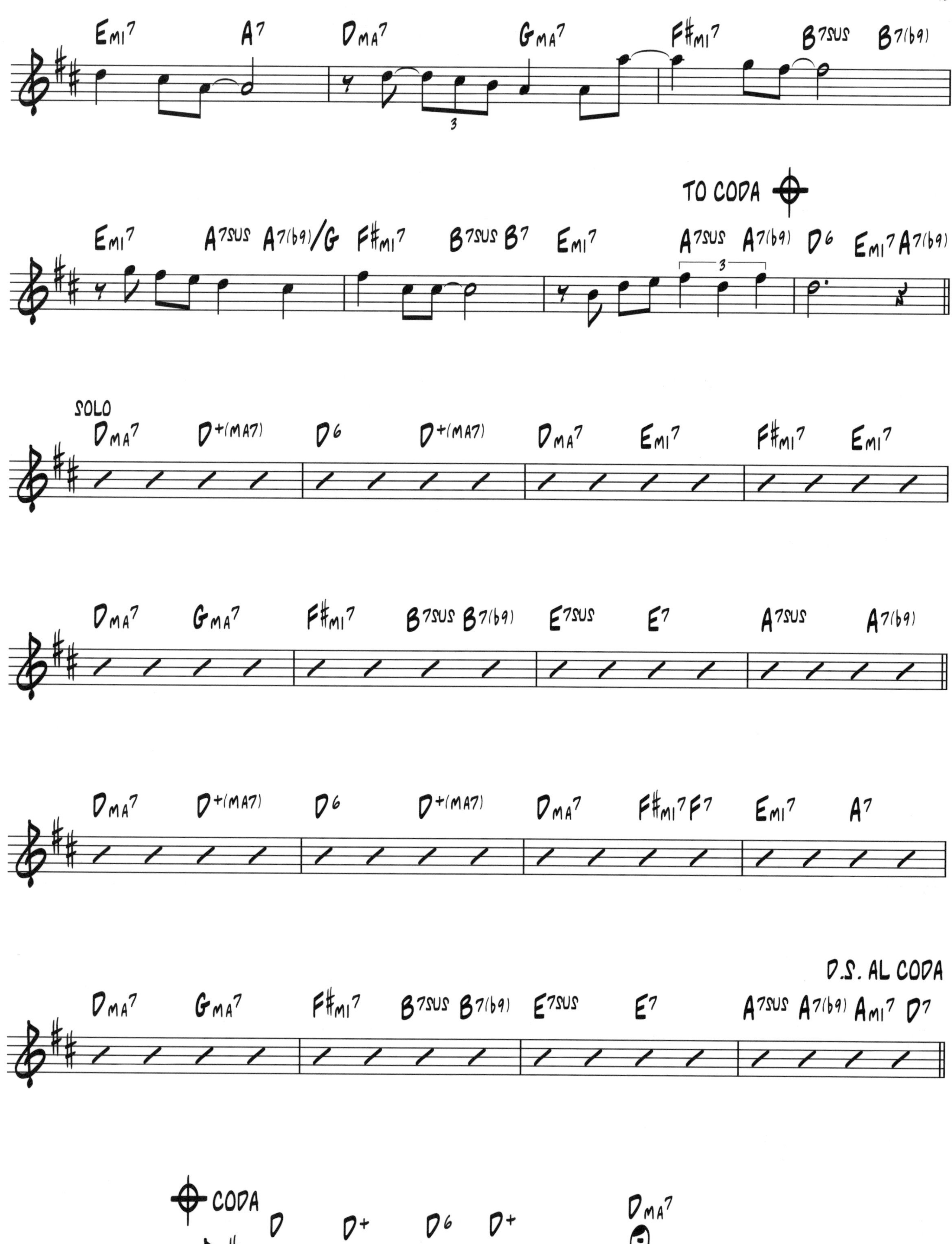
EMI7 A7 DMA7 GMA7 F#MI7 B7SUS B7(b9)
3
TO CODA
EMI7 A7SUS A7(b9)/G F#MI7 B7SUS B7 EMI7 A7SUS A7(b9) D6 EMI7 A7(b9)
3
SOLO
DMA7 D+(MA7) D6 D+(MA7) DMA7 EMI7 F#MI7 EMI7
DMA7 GMA7 F#MI7 B7SUS B7(b9) E7SUS E7 A7SUS A7(b9)
DMA7 D+(MA7) D6 D+(MA7) DMA7 F#MI7 F7 EMI7 A7
D.S. AL CODA
DMA7 GMA7 F#MI7 B7SUS B7(b9) E7SUS E7 A7SUS A7(b9) AMI7 D7
CODA
D D+ D6 D+ DMA7
RIT.

CD

11: SPLIT TRACK/MELODY

12: FULL STEREO TRACK

MAKE SOMEONE HAPPY

FROM DO RE MI

WORDS BY BETTY COMDEN AND ADOLPH GREEN
MUSIC BY JULE STYNE

E♭ VERSION

BOSSA

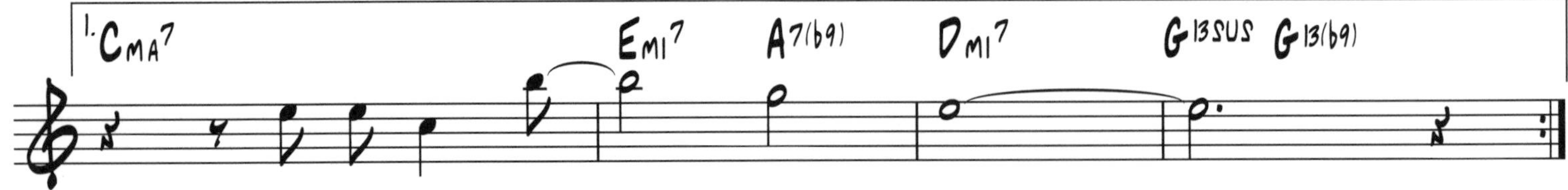

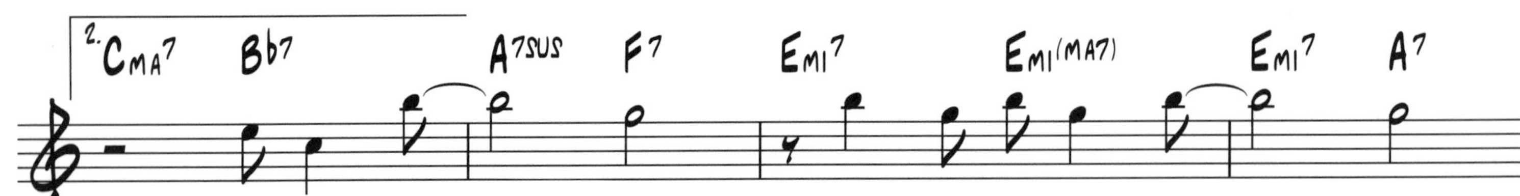

TO CODA
DMI7 EMI7 FMA7 G7SUS G7(b9) E+7(b9) Eb13 DMI9 G13(b9)
SOLO
C C+ C6 CMA7 C C+ C6 CMA7
GMI7 GMI(MA7) GMI7 GMI6 GMI7 C7SUS C7(b9)
FMA7 F+ F6 FMA7 FMI7 Bb7 G7(b9)
1.
CMA7 EMI7 A7(b9) DMI7 G13(b9)
2.
CMA7 Bb7 A7SUS F7 EMI7 EMI(MA7) EMI7 A7
D.S. AL CODA
CODA
FMA7 Eb7 DMI7 G7SUS FMA7 Eb7 DMI7 G7SUS
FMA7 Eb7 DMI7 C#MA7(b5) CMA7(b5)

CD

13: SPLIT TRACK/MELODY

14: FULL STEREO TRACK

OLD DEVIL MOON

FROM FINIAN'S RAINBOW

WORDS BY E.Y. HARBURG
MUSIC BY BURTON LANE

E♭ VERSION

LATIN

D7 C7 D7 C7

LATIN

D7 C7 D7 C7

mf

SWING

GMA7 C7(♭5)

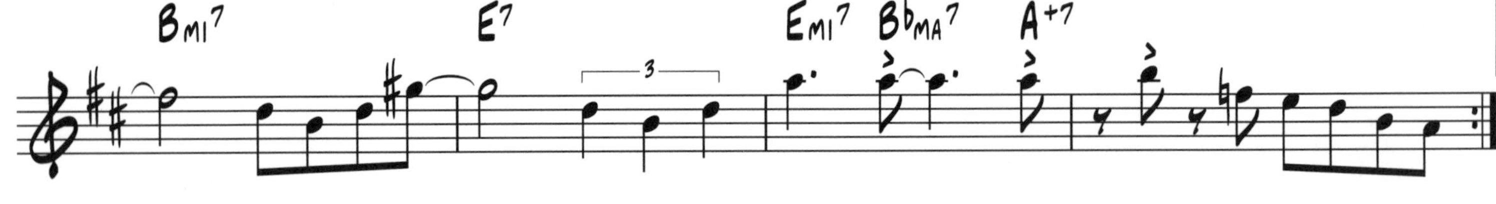

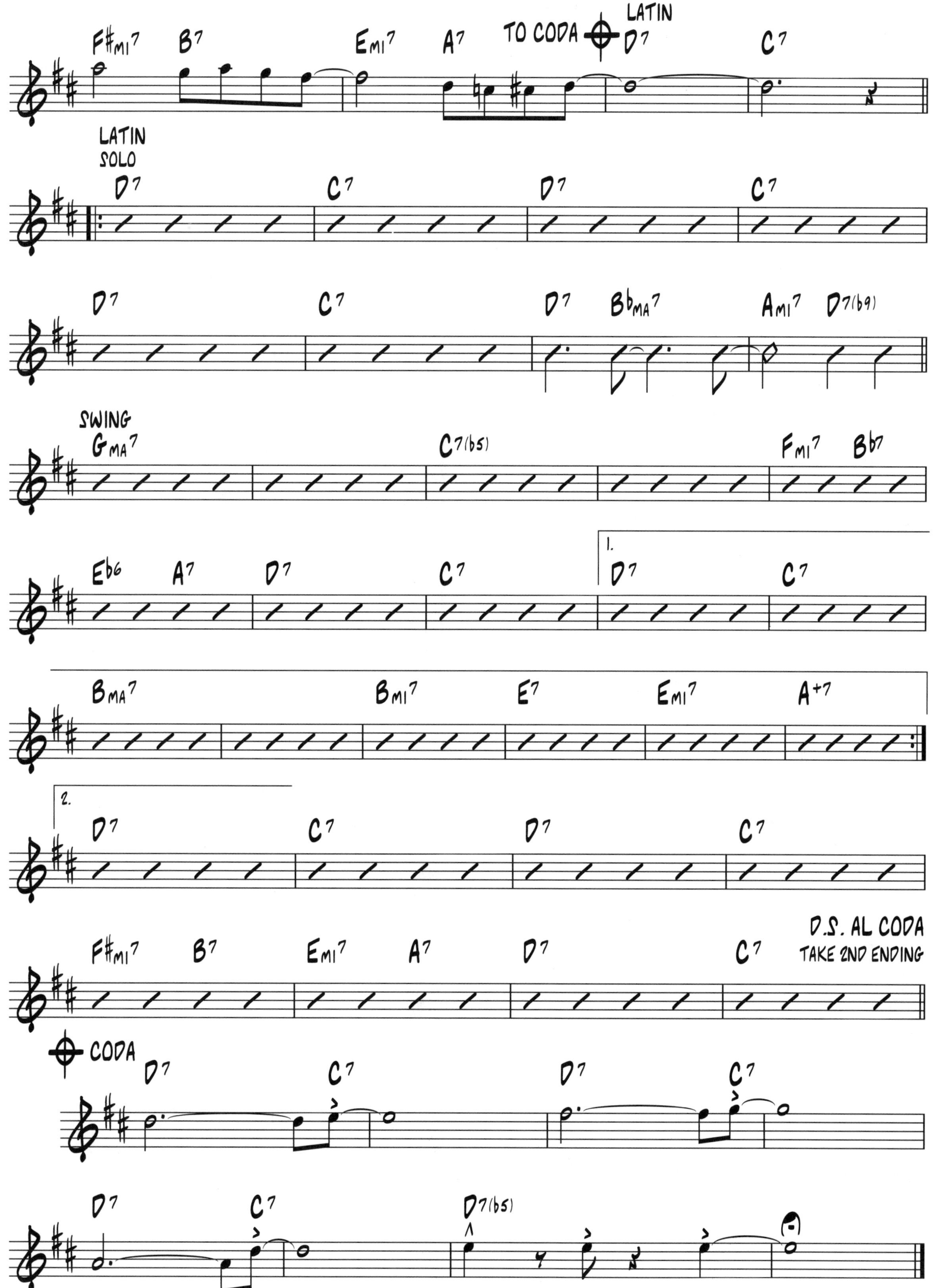
F♯MI7
B7
EMI7
A7
TO CODA
LATIN
D7
C7
LATIN
SOLO
D7
C7
D7
C7
D7
C7
D7
B♭MA7
AMI7
D7(♭9)
SWING
GMA7
C7(♭5)
FMI7
B♭7
E♭6
A7
D7
C7
1.
D7
C7
BMA7
BMI7
E7
EMI7
A+7
2.
D7
C7
D7
C7
F♯MI7
B7
EMI7
A7
D7
C7
D.S. AL CODA
TAKE 2ND ENDING
CODA
D7
C7
D7
C7
D7
C7
D7(♭5)

CD

15: SPLIT TRACK/MELODY
16: FULL STEREO TRACK

SMALL WORLD

FROM GYPSY

WORDS BY STEPHEN SONDHEIM
MUSIC BY JULE STYNE

E♭ VERSION

SOFT LATIN

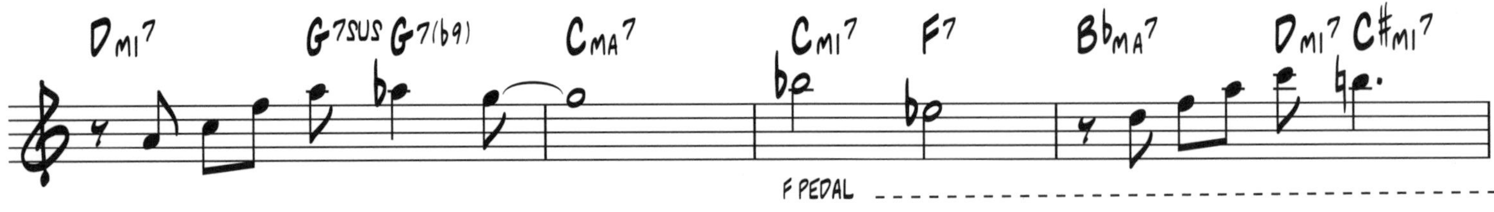

C6/9
Dmi7/C
C6/9
Emi7/B
Bb07
Dmi7/A
G7SUS
Emi7
A7SUS
A7
D7 SUS
D7
G7 SUS
G7
TO CODA
C6/9
C#6/9
SOLO
C6/9
Dmi7/C
C6/9
Dmi7/C
C6/9
G#7(b5)
G7SUS
C6/9
Dmi7/C
C6/9
1.
Emi7/B
Bb07
Dmi7/A
G7SUS
2.
Emi7
A7SUS
A7
D.S. AL CODA
CODA
C6/9
C#6/9
C6/9
C#6/9
C#MA7(b5)
CMA7(b5)
RIT.

17: SPLIT TRACK/MELODY
18: FULL STEREO TRACK

TILL THERE WAS YOU

FROM MEREDITH WILLSON'S THE MUSIC MAN

BY MEREDITH WILLSON

E♭ VERSION

SOLO
CMA7 C#07 DMI7 FMI7 Bb7
CMA7 D#07 DMI7 G7
1.
EMI7 Eb7 DMI7 G7
2.
C6 Bb7 B7(b9) CMA7 FMA7 F#07 CMA7/G
EMI7 A7(b9) DMI7 AMI7 D7 DMI7 G+7
CMA7 C#07 DMI7 FMI7 Bb7
D.S. AL CODA
CMA7 D#07 DMI7 G7 C6 Bb7 B7(b9) CMA7
CODA
C6 AMI7 DMI7 G7 C#7 CMA7

CD

19: SPLIT TRACK/MELODY
20: FULL STEREO TRACK

TOO CLOSE FOR COMFORT

FROM THE MUSICAL MR. WONDERFUL

WORDS AND MUSIC BY JERRY BOCK,
LARRY HOLOFCENER AND GEORGE WEISS

E♭ VERSION

SWING A6/9 G♯+7 C♯MI7(♭5) F♯7
mf
BMI7(♭5) E7(♭9) 1. AMA7 F♯MI7 BMI7 E7(♭9)
2. F°7 EMI7 A7(♭9) D7 D♯°7
A6/E EMI7 A7(♭9) D7 D♯°7
A6/E F7 E7SUS E7(♭9) 𝄋 A6/9 G♯+7
C♯MI7(♭5) F♯7 BMI7(♭5) E7(♭9) AMA7
F°7 EMI7 A7(♭9) D7 D♯°7
TO CODA
F♯MI7(♭5) B7(♭9) F7 E7(♭9) A6/9

SOLO BREAK
SOLO (2 CHORUSES)
A6/9
G#+7
C#MI7(b5)
F#7
BMI7(b5)
E7(b9)
1.
A6
F#MI7
BMI7
E7(b9)
2.
A6
F07
EMI7
A7(b9)
D7
D#07
A6/E
EMI7
A7(b9)
D7
D#07
A6/E
F7
E7SUS
E7(b9)
A6/9
G#+7
C#MI7(b5)
F#7
BMI7(b5)
E7(b9)
A6
F07
EMI7
A7(b9)
D7
D#07
F#MI7(b5)
B7(b9)
D.S. AL CODA
F7
E7(b9)
A6/9
E7SUS
E7(b9)
CODA
AMA13(#11)

CD

7 : SPLIT TRACK/MELODY
8 : FULL STEREO TRACK

E♭ VERSION

I'VE GROWN ACCUSTOMED TO HER FACE

FROM MY FAIR LADY

WORDS BY ALAN JAY LERNER
MUSIC BY FREDERICK LOEWE

CD
7 : SPLIT TRACK/MELODY
8 : FULL STEREO TRACK

I'VE GROWN ACCUSTOMED TO HER FACE

FROM MY FAIR LADY

WORDS BY ALAN JAY LERNER
MUSIC BY FREDERICK LOEWE

𝄢 C VERSION

BALLAD
Eb MA7 Ab7 GMI7 CMI7 FMI7 Cb7 Bb7SUS Bb7
mp
AbMA7(b5) AMI7(b5) D7(b9) GMI7 C7(b9) FMI7 GMI7 Ab6 Bb7
EbMA7 Ab7 GMI7 CMI7 FMI7 Cb7 Bb7SUS A7(b5)
𝄋 AbMA7 AMI7(b5) D+7(b9) GMI7 C+7 FMI7 Bb7 G+7 C+7
TO CODA
AMI7(b5) AbMI7 GMI7 C7(b9) FMI7 Bb7SUS Eb6 Bb7SUS Bb7(b9)
SOLO
EbMA7 Ab7 GMI7 CMI7 FMI7 Cb7 Bb7SUS Bb7
AbMA7(b5) AMI7(b5) D7(b9) GMI7 C7(b9) FMI7 GMI7 Ab6 Bb7
D.S. AL CODA
EbMA7 Ab7 GMI7 CMI7 FMI7 Cb7 Bb7SUS A7(b5)
CODA AbMA7 G+7 Gb7 FMI7 E7 EbMA7
RIT.

AIN'T MISBEHAVIN'

FROM AIN'T MISBEHAVIN'

WORDS BY ANDY RAZAF
MUSIC BY THOMAS "FATS" WALLER AND
HARRY BROOKS

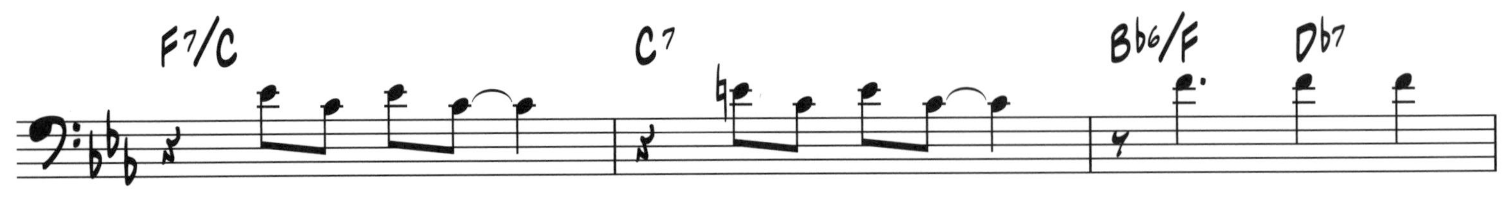

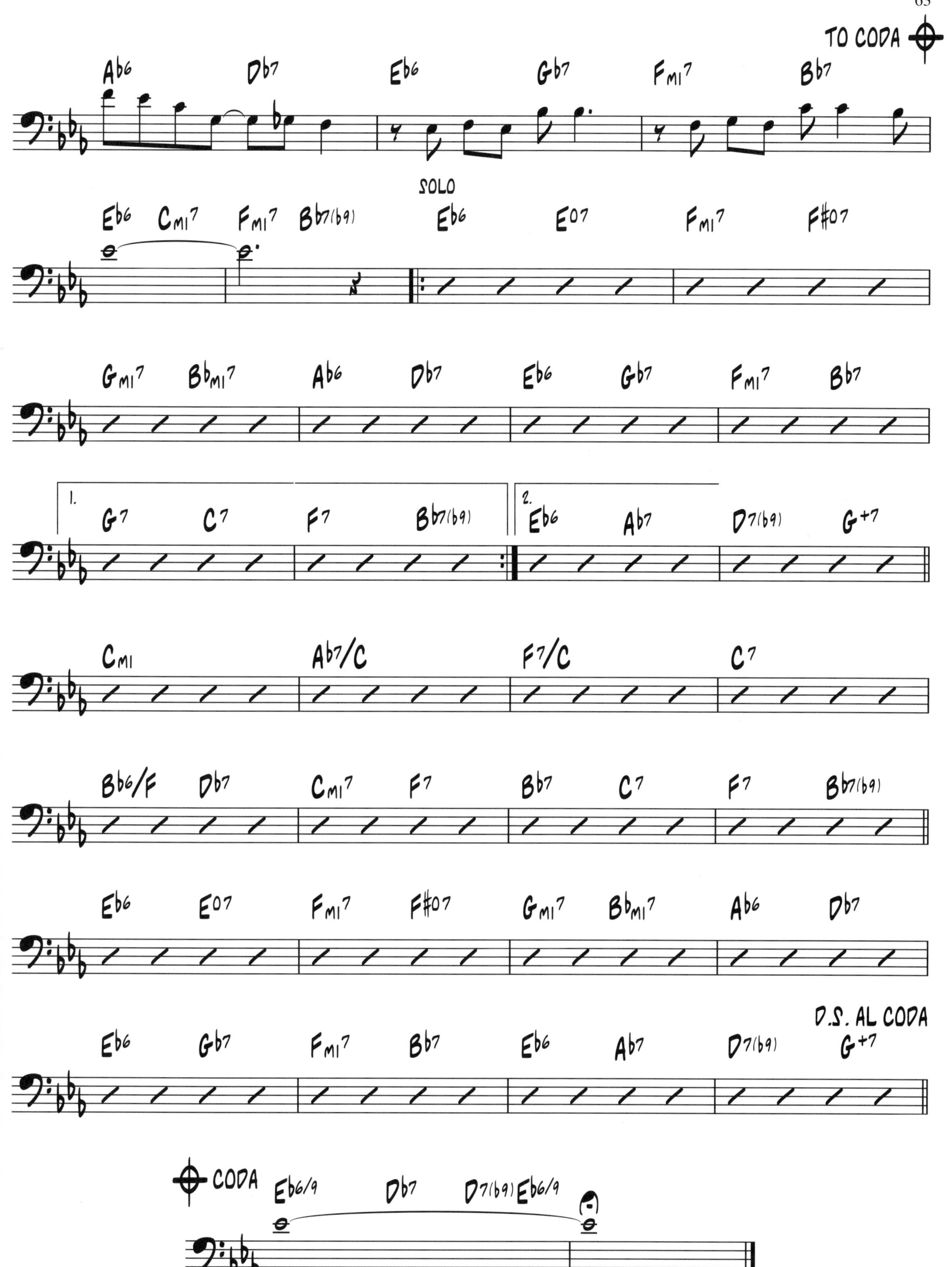
TO CODA
Ab6 Db7 Eb6 Gb7 Fmi7 Bb7
SOLO
Eb6 Cmi7 Fmi7 Bb7(b9) Eb6 E°7 Fmi7 F#°7
Gmi7 Bbmi7 Ab6 Db7 Eb6 Gb7 Fmi7 Bb7
1.
G7 C7 F7 Bb7(b9)
2.
Eb6 Ab7 D7(b9) G+7
Cmi Ab7/C F7/C C7
Bb6/F Db7 Cmi7 F7 Bb7 C7 F7 Bb7(b9)
Eb6 E°7 Fmi7 F#°7 Gmi7 Bbmi7 Ab6 Db7
D.S. AL CODA
Eb6 Gb7 Fmi7 Bb7 Eb6 Ab7 D7(b9) G+7
CODA
Eb6/9 Db7 D7(b9) Eb6/9

CD

3: SPLIT TRACK/MELODY
4: FULL STEREO TRACK

GET ME TO THE CHURCH ON TIME

FROM MY FAIR LADY

WORDS BY ALAN JAY LERNER
MUSIC BY FREDERICK LOEWE

C VERSION

BMI7 E7(b9) AMI7 CMI7 F7

BMI7 Bb7 AMI7 G6/B CMA7 A7/C# D7SUS D7(b9)

TO CODA

G6 SOLO BREAK

SOLO

GMA7 G6/9 GMA7 G6/9

GMA7 G6/9 GMA7 G#O7 AMI7 D7 AMI7 D7

BMI7 Bb7 A+7 Ab7

1\. GMA7 G6/9

2\. G6 CMA7

GMA7 EMI7 A7 AMI7 D7 GMA7 G6/9

GMA7 G6/9 GMA7 G6/9 GMA7 G#O7 AMI7 D7

BMI7 E7(b9) AMI7 CMI7 F7 BMI7 Bb7

D.C. AL CODA

TAKE REPEAT

AMI7 G6/B CMA7 A7/C# D7SUS D7(b9) D7SUS D7(b9)

CODA

G6 Ab6/9 GMA7

CD

I LOVE PARIS

FROM CAN-CAN
FROM HIGH SOCIETY

WORDS AND MUSIC
BY COLE PORTER

C VERSION

SOFT SAMBA

G+7

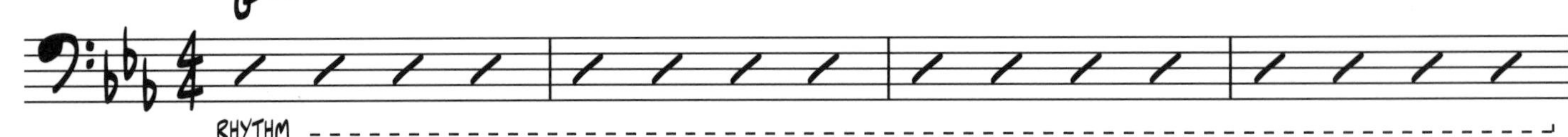

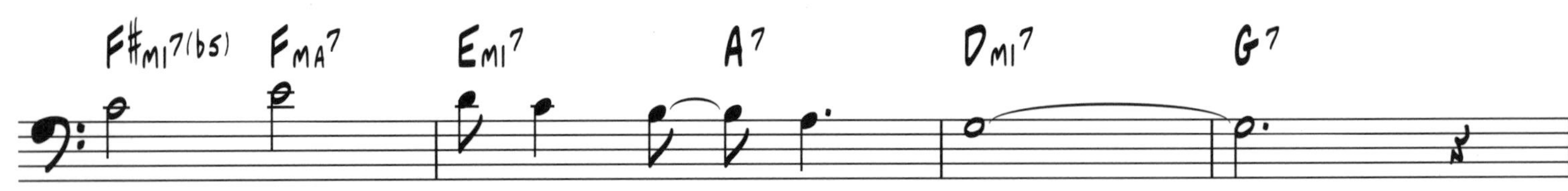

TO CODA
DMI7 G7SUS G7(b9) C6 DMI7(b5) G+7
SOLO
CMI Ab/C CMI6 CMI7 CMI(MA7) CMI7 CMI6 Ab/C
CMI CMI/Bb A°7 Ab7 G7SUS G7(b9)
DMI7(b5) G7(b9) DMI7(b5) G7(b9)
DMI7(b5) Ab7 G7SUS G+7(b9) CMI6 CMI G7SUS
CMA7 FMA7/C CMA7 FMA7/C
F#MI7(b5) FMA7 EMI7 A7 DMI7 G7
FMA7 F#°7 B7(b9) EMI7 FMA7 EMI7 A7
D.S. AL CODA
DMI7 G7SUS G7(b9) C6 DMI7(b5) G+7
CODA
CMI Ab/C CMI6 CMI7 CMI(MA7) CMI7 CMI6 Ab/C CMI6/9

CD

9 : SPLIT TRACK/MELODY

10 : FULL STEREO TRACK

IT NEVER ENTERED MY MIND

FROM HIGHER AND HIGHER

WORDS LORENZ HART
MUSIC BY RICHARD RODGERS

BALLAD

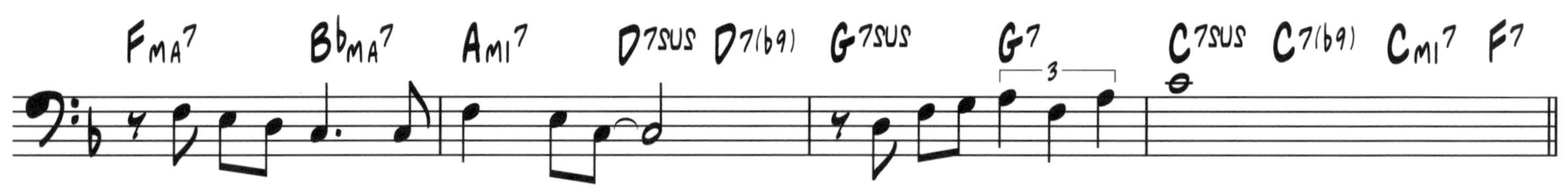

GMI7 C7 FMA7 BbMA7 AMI7 D7SUS D7(b9)
TO CODA
GMI7 C7SUS C7(b9)/Bb AMI7 D7SUS D7 GMI7 C7SUS C7(b9) F6 GMI7 C7(b9)
SOLO
FMA7 F+(MA7) F6 F+(MA7) FMA7 GMI7 AMI7 GMI7
FMA7 BbMA7 AMI7 D7SUS D7(b9) G7SUS G7 C7SUS C7(b9)
FMA7 F+(MA7) F6 F+(MA7) FMA7 AMI7 Ab7 GMI7 C7
D.S. AL CODA
FMA7 BbMA7 AMI7 D7SUS D7(b9) G7SUS G7 C7SUS C7(b9) CMI7 F7
CODA
F F+ F6 F+ FMA7
RIT.

CD

MAKE SOMEONE HAPPY

FROM DO RE MI

WORDS BY BETTY COMDEN AND ADOLPH GREEN
MUSIC BY JULE STYNE

C VERSION

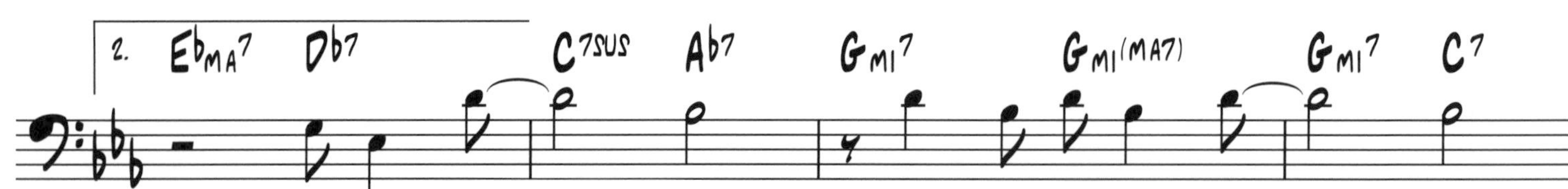

TO CODA
FMI7 GMI7 AbMA7 Bb7SUS Bb7(b9) G+7(b9) Gb13 FMI9 Bb13(b9)
SOLO
Eb Eb+ Eb6 EbMA7 Eb Eb+ Eb6 EbMA7
BbMI7 BbMI(MA7) BbMI7 BbMI6 BbMI7 Eb7SUS Eb7(b9)
AbMA7 Ab+ Ab6 AbMA7 AbMI7 Db7 Bb7(b9)
1.
EbMA7 GMI7 C7(b9) FMI7 Bb13(b9)
D.S. AL CODA
2.
EbMA7 Db7 C7SUS Ab7 GMI7 GMI(MA7) GMI7 C7
CODA
AbMA7 Gb7 FMI7 Bb7SUS AbMA7 Gb7 FMI7 Bb7SUS
AbMA7 Gb7 FMI7 EMA7(b5) EbMA7(b5)

CD

13: SPLIT TRACK/MELODY
14: FULL STEREO TRACK

OLD DEVIL MOON

FROM FINIAN'S RAINBOW

WORDS BY E.Y. HARBURG
MUSIC BY BURTON LANE

C VERSION

LATIN

mf

SWING

TO CODA
LATIN
Ami7
D7
Gmi7
C7
F7
Eb7
LATIN
SOLO
F7
Eb7
F7
Eb7
F7
Eb7
F7
Dbma7
Cmi7
F7(b9)
SWING
Bbma7
Eb7(b5)
Abmi7
Db7
Gb6
C7
F7
Eb7
1.
F7
Eb7
Dma7
Dmi7
G7
Gmi7
C+7
2.
F7
Eb7
F7
Eb7
D.S. AL CODA
TAKE 2ND ENDING
Ami7
D7
Gmi7
C7
F7
Eb7
CODA
F7
Eb7
F7
Eb7
F7
Eb7
F7(b5)

CD

15 : SPLIT TRACK/MELODY

16 : FULL STEREO TRACK

SMALL WORLD

FROM GYPSY

WORDS BY STEPHEN SONDHEIM
MUSIC BY JULE STYNE

C VERSION

SOFT LATIN

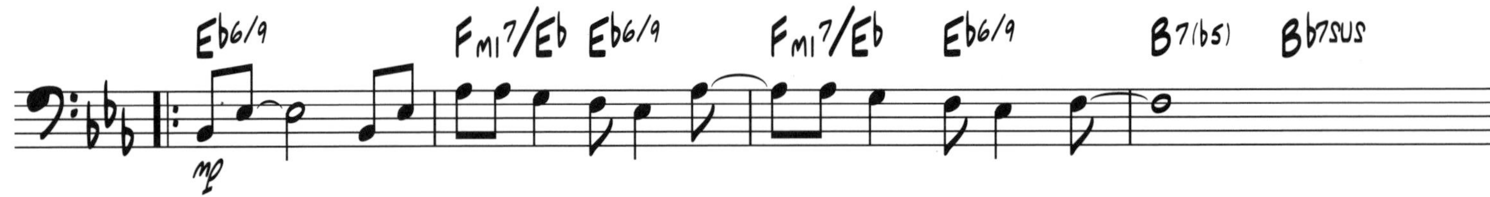

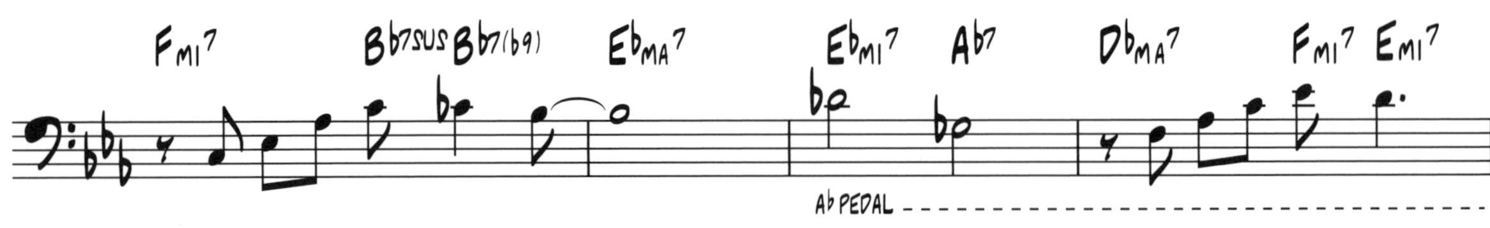

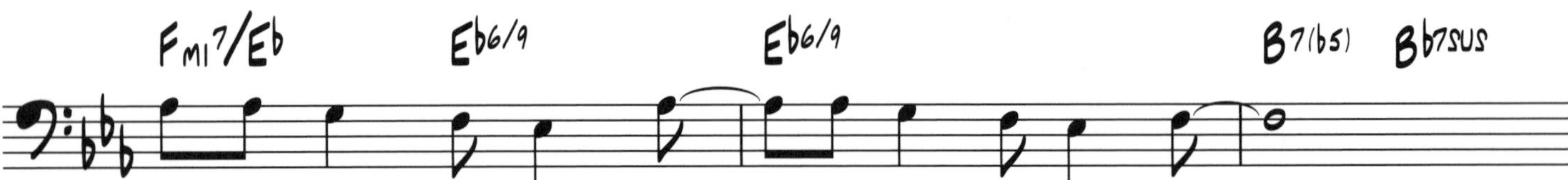

Eb6/9
Fmi7/Eb
Eb6/9
Gmi7/D Db07
Fmi7/C
Bb7sus
Gmi7
C7sus
C7
TO CODA
F7 sus
F7
Bb7 sus
Bb7
Eb6/9
E6/9
SOLO
Eb6/9
Fmi7/Eb
Eb6/9
Fmi7/Eb
Eb6/9
B7(b5)
Bb7sus
Eb6/9
Fmi7/Eb
Eb6/9
1.
Gmi7/D
Db07
Fmi7/C
Bb7sus
2.
Gmi7
C7sus
C7
D.S. AL CODA
CODA
Eb6/9
E6/9
Eb6/9
E6/9
Ema7(b5)
Ebma7(b5)
RIT.

CD

17 : SPLIT TRACK/MELODY
18 : FULL STEREO TRACK

TILL THERE WAS YOU

FROM MEREDITH WILLSON'S THE MUSIC MAN

BY MEREDITH WILLSON

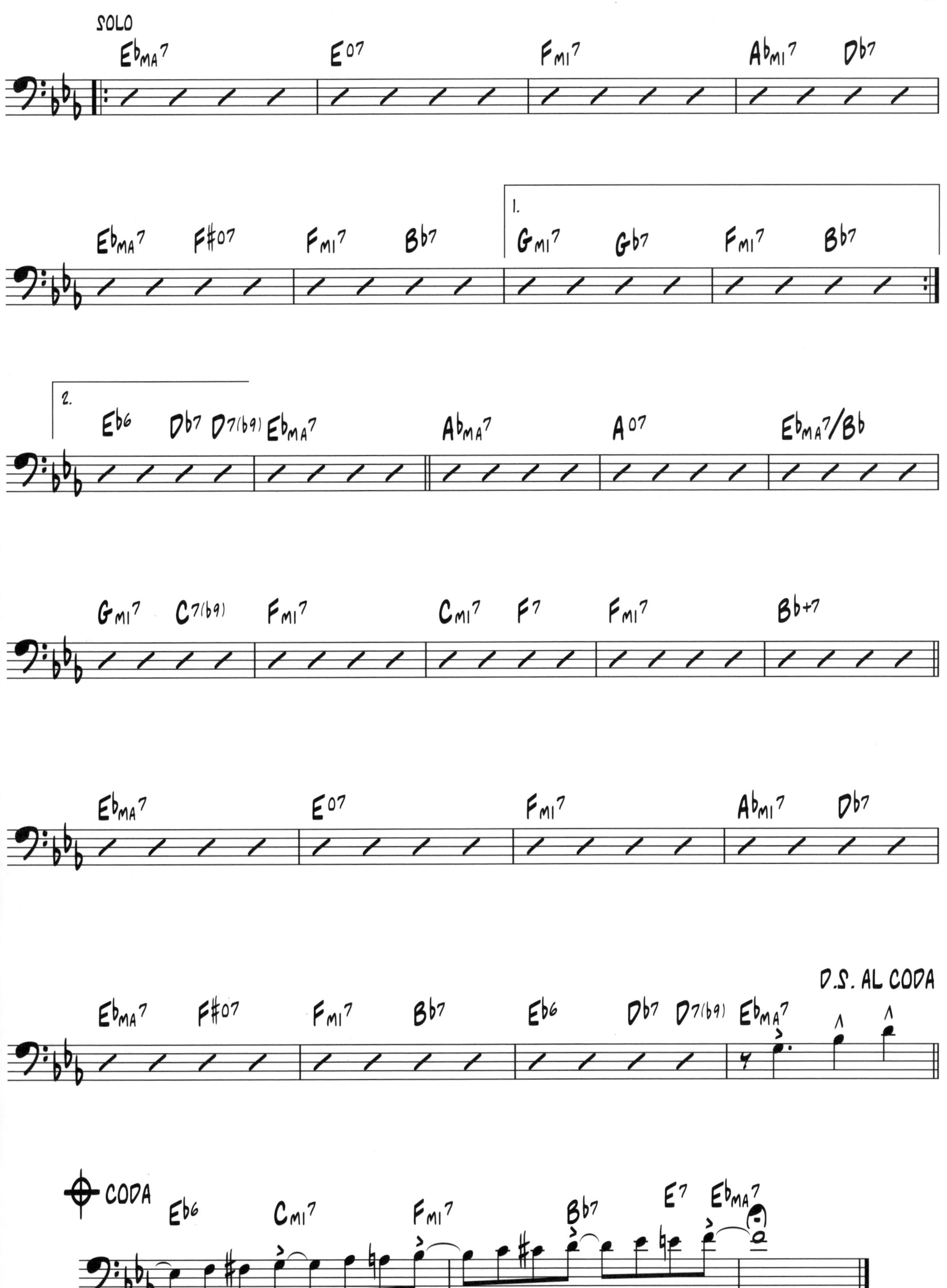
SOLO
Ebma7
E07
Fmi7
Abmi7
Db7
1.
Ebma7
F#07
Fmi7
Bb7
Gmi7
Gb7
Fmi7
Bb7
2.
Eb6
Db7
D7(b9)
Ebma7
Abma7
A07
Ebma7/Bb
Gmi7
C7(b9)
Fmi7
Cmi7
F7
Fmi7
Bb+7
Ebma7
E07
Fmi7
Abmi7
Db7
D.S. AL CODA
Ebma7
F#07
Fmi7
Bb7
Eb6
Db7
D7(b9)
Ebma7
CODA
Eb6
Cmi7
Fmi7
Bb7
E7
Ebma7

CD

19 : SPLIT TRACK/MELODY
20 : FULL STEREO TRACK

TOO CLOSE FOR COMFORT

FROM THE MUSICAL MR. WONDERFUL

WORDS AND MUSIC BY JERRY BOCK,
LARRY HOLOFCENER AND GEORGE WEISS

C VERSION

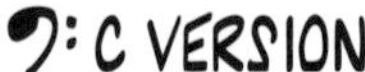

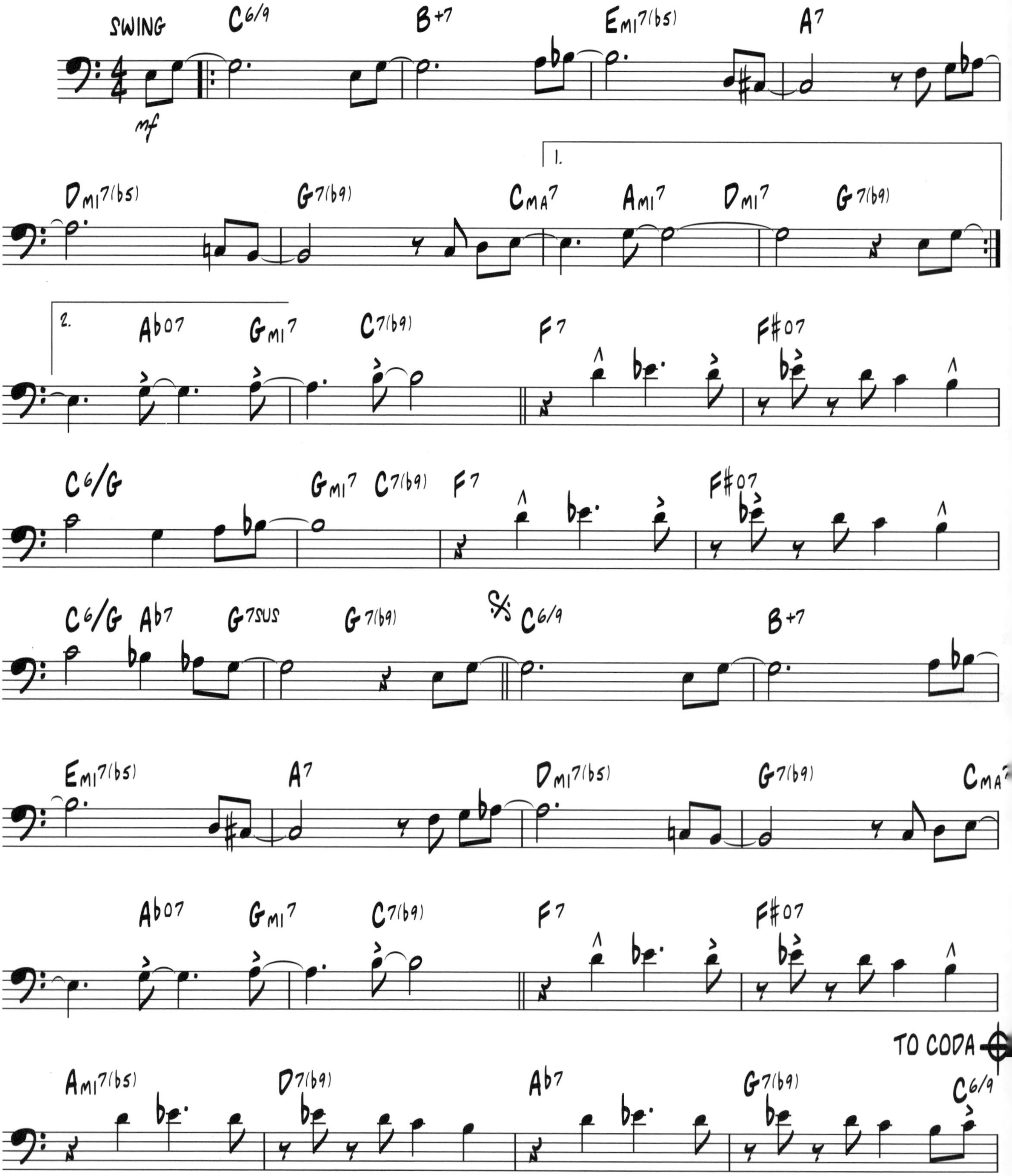
SWING
C6/9
B+7
Emi7(b5)
A7
mf
Dmi7(b5)
G7(b9)
1.
Cma7
Ami7
Dmi7
G7(b9)
2.
Abo7
Gmi7
C7(b9)
F7
F#o7
C6/G
Gmi7
C7(b9)
F7
F#o7
C6/G
Ab7
G7sus
G7(b9)
C6/9
B+7
Emi7(b5)
A7
Dmi7(b5)
G7(b9)
Cma7
Abo7
Gmi7
C7(b9)
F7
F#o7
TO CODA
Ami7(b5)
D7(b9)
Ab7
G7(b9)
C6/9

SOLO BREAK
SOLO (2 CHORUSES)
C6/9
B+7
EMI7(b5)
A7
DMI7(b5)
G7(b9)
1.
C6
AMI7
DMI7
G7(b9)
2.
C6
Ab07
GMI7
C7(b9)
F7
F#07
C6/G
GMI7
C7(b9)
F7
F#07
C6/G
Ab7
G7SUS
G7(b9)
C6/9
B+7
EMI7(b5)
A7
DMI7(b5)
G7(b9)
C6
Ab07
GMI7
C7(b9)
F7
F#07
AMI7(b5)
D7(b9)
Ab7
G7(b9)
C6/9
G7SUS
G7(b9)
D.S. AL CODA
CODA
CMA13(#11)

Presenting the Hal Leonard JAZZ PLAY ALONG SERIES

DUKE ELLINGTON Vol. 1 00841644
Caravan • Don't Get Around Much Anymore • In a Mellow Tone • In a Sentimental Mood • It Don't Mean a Thing (If It Ain't Got That Swing) • Perdido • Prelude to a Kiss • Satin Doll • Sophisticated Lady • Take the "A" Train.

MILES DAVIS Vol. 2 00841645
All Blues • Blue in Green • Four • Half Nelson • Milestones • Nardis • Seven Steps to Heaven • So What • Solar • Tune Up.

THE BLUES Vol. 3 00841646
Billie's Bounce • Birk's Works • Blues for Alice • Blues in the Closet • C-Jam Blues • Freddie Freeloader • Mr. P.C. • Now's the Time • Tenor Madness • Things Ain't What They Used to Be.

JAZZ BALLADS Vol. 4 00841691
Body and Soul • But Beautiful • Here's That Rainy Day • Misty • My Foolish Heart • My Funny Valentine • My One and Only Love • My Romance • The Nearness of You • Polka Dots and Moonbeams.

BEST OF BEBOP Vol. 5 00841689
Anthropology • Donna Lee • Doxy • Epistrophy • Lady Bird • Oleo • Ornithology • Scrapple from the Apple • Woodyn' You • Yardbird Suite.

JAZZ CLASSICS WITH EASY CHANGES Vol. 6 00841690
Blue Train • Comin' Home Baby • Footprints • Impressions • Killer Joe • Moanin' • Sidewinder • St. Thomas • Stolen Moments • Well You Needn't.

ESSENTIAL JAZZ STANDARDS Vol. 7 00843000
Autumn Leaves • Cotton Tail • Easy Living • I Remember You • If I Should Lose You • Lullaby of Birdland • Out of Nowhere • Stella by Starlight • There Will Never Be Another You • When Sunny Gets Blue.

ANTONIO CARLOS JOBIM AND THE ART OF THE BOSSA NOVA Vol. 8 00843001
The Girl from Ipanema • How Insensitive • Meditation • Once I Loved • One Note Samba • Quiet Nights of Quiet Stars • Slightly Out of Tune • So Danco Samba • Triste • Wave.

DIZZY GILLESPIE Vol. 9 00843002
Birk's Works • Con Alma • Groovin' High • Manteca • A Night in Tunisia • Salt Peanuts • Shawnuff • Things to Come • Tour De Force • Woodyn' You.

DISNEY CLASSICS Vol. 10 00843003
Alice in Wonderland • Beauty and the Beast • Cruella De Vil • Heigh-Ho • Some Day My Prince Will Come • When You Wish upon a Star • Whistle While You Work • Who's Afraid of the Big Bad Wolf • You've Got a Friend in Me • Zip-a-Dee-Doo-Dah.

RODGERS AND HART FAVORITES Vol. 11 00843004
Bewitched • The Blue Room • Dancing on the Ceiling • Have You Met Miss Jones? • I Could Write a Book • The Lady Is a Tramp • Little Girl Blue • My Romance • There's a Small Hotel • You Are Too Beautiful.

ESSENTIAL JAZZ CLASSICS Vol. 12 00843005
Airegin • Ceora • The Frim Fram Sauce • Israel • Milestones • Nefertiti • Red Clay • Satin Doll • Song for My Father • Take Five.

JOHN COLTRANE Vol. 13 00843006
Blue Train • Countdown • Cousin Mary • Equinox • Giant Steps • Impressions • Lazy Bird • Mr. P.C. • Moment's Notice • Naima.

IRVING BERLIN Vol. 14 00843007
Be Careful, It's My Heart • Blue Skies • Change Partners • Cheek to Cheek • How Deep Is the Ocean • I've Got My Love to Keep Me Warm • Let's Face the Music and Dance • Steppin' Out with My Baby • They Say It's Wonderful • What'll I Do?

RODGERS & HAMMERSTEIN Vol. 15 00843008
Bali Ha'i • Do I Love You Because You're Beautiful? • Hello Young Lovers • I Have Dreamed • It Might as Well Be Spring • Love, Look Away • My Favorite Things • The Surrey with the Fringe on Top • The Sweetest Sounds • Younger Than Springtime.

COLE PORTER Vol. 16 00843009
All of You • At Long Last • Easy to Love • Ev'ry Time We Say Goodbye • I Concentrate on You • I've Got You Under My Skin • In the Still of the Night • It's All Right with Me • It's De-Lovely • You'd Be So Nice to Come Home To.

COUNT BASIE Vol. 17 00843010
All of Me • April in Paris • Blues in Hoss Flat • Cute • Jumpin' at the Woodside • Li'l Darlin' • Moten Swing • One O'Clock Jump • Shiny Stockings • Until I Met You.

HAROLD ARLEN Vol. 18 00843011
Ac-cent-tchu-ate the Positive • Between the Devil and the Deep Blue Sea • Come Rain or Come Shine • If I Only Had a Brain • It's Only a Paper Moon • I've Got the World on a String • My Shining Hour • Over the Rainbow • Stormy Weather • That Old Black Magic.

COOL JAZZ Vol. 19 00843012
Bernie's Tune • Boplicity • Budo • Conception • Django • Five Brothers • Line for Lyons • Walkin' Shoes • Waltz for Debby • Whisper Not.

RODGERS AND HART CLASSICS Vol. 21 00843014
Falling in Love with Love • Isn't it Romantic? • Manhattan • Mountain Greenery • My Funny Valentine • My Heart Stood Still • This Can't Be Love • Thou Swell • Where or When • You Took Advantage of Me.

WAYNE SHORTER Vol. 22 00843015
Children of the Night • ESP • Footprints • Juju • Mahjong • Nefertiti • Nightdreamer • Speak No Evil • Witch Hunt • Yes and No.

LATIN JAZZ Vol. 23 00843016
Agua De Beber • Chega De Saudade • The Gift! • Invitation • Manha De Carnaval • Mas Que Nada • Ran Kan Kan • So Nice • Sweet Happy Life • Watch What Happens.

EARLY JAZZ STANDARDS Vol. 24 00843017
After You've Gone • Avalon • Indian Summer • Indiana (Back Home Again in Indiana) • Ja-Da • Limehouse Blues • Paper Doll • Poor Butterfly • Rose Room • St. Louis Blues.

CHRISTMAS JAZZ Vol. 25 00843018
The Christmas Song (Chestnuts Roasting on an Open Fire) • The Christmas Waltz • Frosty the Snow Man • Home for the Holidays • I Heard the Bells on Christmas Day • I'll Be Home for Christmas • Let It Snow! Let It Snow! Let It Snow! • Rudolph the Red-Nosed Reindeer • Silver Bells • Snowfall.

CHARLIE PARKER Vol. 26 00843019
Au Privave • Billie's Bounce • Confirmation • Donna Lee • Moose the Mooche • My Little Suede Shoes • Now's the Time • Ornithology • Scrapple from the Apple • Yardbird Suite.

GREAT JAZZ STANDARDS Vol. 27 00843020
Fly Me to the Moon • Girl Talk • How High the Moon • I Can't Get Started with You • It Could Happen to You • Lover • Softly As in a Morning Sunrise • Speak Low • Tangerine • Willow Weep for Me.

BIG BAND ERA Vol. 28 00843021
Air Mail Special • Christopher Columbus • Four Brothers • In the Mood • Intermission Riff • Jersey Bounce • Opus One • Stompin' at the Savoy • A String of Pearls • Tuxedo Junction.

LENNON AND MCCARTNEY Vol. 29 00843022
And I Love Her • Blackbird • Come Together • Eleanor Rigby • The Fool on the Hill • Here, There and Everywhere • Lady Madonna • Let It Be • Ticket to Ride • Yesterday.

BLUES' BEST Vol. 30 00843023
Basin Street Blues • Bloomdido • D Natural Blues • Everyday I Have the Blues Again • Happy Go Lucky Local • K.C. Blues • Sonnymoon for Two • The Swingin' Shepherd Blues • Take the Coltrane • Turnaround • Twisted.

JAZZ IN THREE Vol. 31 00843024
Bluesette • Gravy Waltz • Jitterbug Waltz • Moon River • Oh, What a Beautiful Mornin' • Tenderly • Tennessee Waltz • West Coast Blues • What the World Needs Now Is Love • Wives and Lovers.

BEST OF SWING Vol. 32 00843025
Alright, Okay, You Win • Cherokee • I'll Be Seeing You • I've Heard That Song Before • Jump, Jive An' Wail • On the Sunny Side of the Street • Route 66 • Sentimental Journey • Seven Come Eleven • What's New?

SONNY ROLLINS Vol. 33 00843029
Airegin • Alfie's Theme • Biji • The Bridge • Doxy • First Moves • Here's to the People • Oleo • St. Thomas • Sonnymoon for Two.

ALL TIME STANDARDS Vol. 34 00843030
Autumn in New York • Broadway • Bye Bye Blackbird • Call Me Irresponsible • Georgia on My Miind • Honeysuckle Rose • I'll Remember April • Stardust • There Is No Greater Love • The Very Thought of You.

BLUESY JAZZ Vol. 35 00843031
Angel Eyes • Bags' Groove • Bessie's Blues • Chitlins Con Carne • Good Morning Heartache • High Fly • Mercy, Mercy, Mercy • Night Train • Sugar • Sweet Georgia Bright.

HORACE SILVER Vol. 36 00843032
Doodlin' • The Jody Grind • Nica's Dream • Opus De Funk • Peace • The Preacher • Senor Blues • Sister Sadie • Song for My Father • Strollin'.

BILL EVANS Vol. 37 00843033
Funkallero • My Bells • One for Helen • The Opener • Orbit • Show-Type Tune • 34 Skidoo • Time Remembered • Turn Out the Stars • Waltz for Debby.

YULETIDE JAZZ Vol. 38 00843034
Blue Christmas • Christmas Time Is Here • Feliz Navidad • Happy Holiday • Here Comes Santa Claus • A Marshmallow World • Merry Christmas, Darling • The Most Wonderful Time of the Year • My Favorite Things • Santa Claus Is Comin' to Town.

ALL THE THINGS YOU ARE & MORE JEROME KERN SONGS Vol. 39 00843035
All the Things You Are • Can't Help Lovin' Dat Man • Dearly Beloved • A Fine Romance • The Folks Who Live on the Hill • Long Ago (And Far Away) • Pick Yourself Up • The Song Is You • The Way You Look Tonight • Yesterday.

BOSSA NOVA Vol. 40 00843036
Black Orpheus • Call Me • Dindi • Little Boat • A Man and a Woman • Only Trust Your Heart • The Shadow of Your Smile • Song of the Jet (Samba do Aviao) • Watch What Happens • Wave.

CLASSIC DUKE ELLINGTON Vol. 41 00843037
C-Jam Blues • Come Sunday • Cotton Tail • Do Nothin' Till You Hear from Me • I Got It Bad and That Ain't Good • I Let a Song Go Out of My Heart • I'm Beginning to See the Light • I'm Just a Lucky So and So • Mood Indigo • Solitude.

JAZZ AT THE MOVIES Vol. 45 00843041
Baby Elephant Walk • God Bless' the Child • The Look of Love • Makin' Whoopee! • More • The Odd Couple • The Rainbow Connection • Swinging on a Star • Thanks for the Memory • Top Hat, White Tie and Tails.

BROADWAY JAZZ STANDARDS Vol. 46 00843042
Ain't Misbehavin' • Get Me to the Church on Time • I Love Paris • I've Grown Accustomed to Her Face • It Never Entered My Mind • Make Someone Happy • Old Devil Moon • Small World • Till There Was You • Too Close for Comfort.

BOOK/CD PACKAGES

ONLY $14.95 EACH!

The Hal Leonard JAZZ PLAY ALONG SERIES is the ultimate learning tool for all jazz musicians. With musician-friendly lead sheets, melody cues and other split track choices on the included CD, this first-of-its-kind package makes learning to play jazz easier and more fun than ever before.

Prices, contents and availability subject to change without notice.

FOR MORE INFORMATION, SEE YOUR LOCAL MUSIC DEALER, OR WRITE TO:

HAL•LEONARD®
CORPORATION
7777 W. BLUEMOUND RD. P.O. BOX 13819
MILWAUKEE, WISCONSIN 53213
Visit Hal Leonard online at
www.halleonard.com

0605

Book and CD for B♭, E♭ and C Instruments

BROADWAY JAZZ STANDARDS

10 MUSICAL THEATRE COMPOSITIONS

Arranged and Produced by Mark Taylor

volume 46

BOOK

CD

ISBN 0-634-09074-7

7777 W. Bluemound Rd. P.O. Box 13819 Milwaukee, WI 53213

Visit Hal Leonard Online at
www.halleonard.com